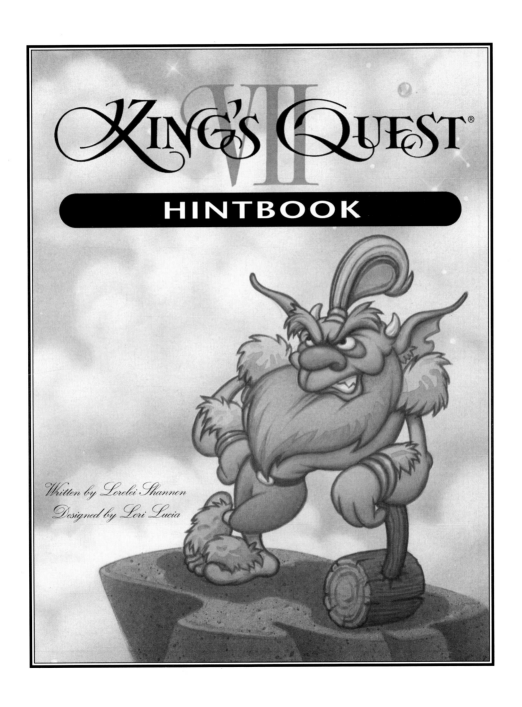

KING'S QUEST VII

HINTBOOK

Written by Lorelei Shannon
Designed by Lori Lucia

Published by Sierra On-Line, Inc.
Oakhurst, California 93644

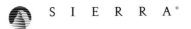

Table of Contents

PART I

I N T R O D U C T I O N

WELCOME TO *KING'S QUEST VII*, IN THIS, SIERRA ON-LINE'S 15TH YEAR! I HAVE TO ADMIT, I REALLY LOVE THIS GAME, AND I THINK YOU WILL TOO. IT HAS FANTASTIC ART, INCREDIBLE ANIMATION, AN EXCELLENT AND INVOLVING STORYLINE, AND TERRIFIC DIALOG. WELL, THAT'S MY (SLIGHTLY BIASED) OPINION AS CO-DESIGNER, ANYWAY. I'M SURE YOU'D RATHER HEAR FROM ROBERTA WILLIAMS...

An Interview with Roberta

Roberta Williams, creator of the King's Quest series.

So the project was finally winding down (at least in the design phase). I invited Roberta out to lunch to talk about the seventh King's Quest game. We were relaxing over pasta and iced lattés, talking about dogs and kids, movies, books and games. We caught up on our chatting (which we're wont to do whenever we get together—just ask Ken), and then it was time to get to work. I pulled out my handy-dandy pocket tape recorder and plunked it on the table. Roberta leaned back in her chair, smiling up at the (rarely) blue Seattle sky as I asked her the first question.

Lorelei: I can't believe the King's Quest series is up to seven! We've come a long way since *Quest for the Crown*. How would you say this King's Quest is different from the KQs that have come before it?

Roberta: This King's Quest has very different animation. I would call it feature-film style, which is a different thing for King's Quest. It also features two protagonists, which is different and unique for the series. Both of them happen to be female, which I think is an interesting twist. I think having female protagonists added a softer, more whimsical approach to the game.

King's Quest I - CGA

King's Quest VII CD

Lorelei: Less bashing and more thinking?

Roberta: Yeah. Less of the macho element. But I think players will find the puzzles just as challenging and fun. Let's see, how else is it different? Well, it's written in chapters, which you can play in any order. You can skip around, like a book. Although *King's Quest VII* has a continuous storyline, each chapter is complete in and of itself. They're almost like little mini-games within the larger game. You also alternate characters with the chapters: You're Valanice, then Rosella, then Valanice, and so on. Of course, they do come together at the end...

Lorelei: So it's more conducive to people's active lifestyles. They're not faced with a huge, endless-looking game; they can actually see goals, and gauge their progress through the chapters.

Roberta: Yes. Absolutely. But it's still a complete, rich storyline, and a long, satisfying game. The story is more compelling than previous King's Quests, and the art is more like an animated feature film than what people think of as "computer art". I think this one will be a hit in the mass market.

Lorelei: One thing that people always seem to notice about King's Quest is that you put a lot of yourself into the game; plenty of fun and humor. What is your favorite part of the game design process?

Roberta: Hmm. I think my favorite part is coming up with the story at the beginning. You know, thinking about what is this story, who is the character, what are they going to do. It's almost like playing a game yourself. Sometimes when you start, you don't know how the design is going to end. It's kind of a weird, vicarious way of playing your own game before anybody else does. (laughs) In fact, after writing these games, I find it anticlimactic to play someone else's adventure game. I'd rather be designing!

Lorelei: Do you have a favorite part of *King's Quest VII?*

Roberta: Give me a minute. I've been so immersed in *Phantasmagoria!** (laughs) Oh, gosh. I think the Troll Underground is so much fun. I like all the trolls; they have a lot of personality. I also like Ooga Booga a lot.

Lorelei: That's my favorite part.

Roberta: (laughs) That figures. I don't know. Maybe I just like the more sinister aspects of the game...

Lorelei: Do I sense a little *Phantasmagoria* creeping in here?

Roberta: That's what it is! Maybe I just got saturated with *Phantasmagoria* and I can't get it out of my head. (laughs) Anyway, those two areas seem to have a little more humor, and they're a little more tongue-in-cheek and quirky than the rest of the game.

*Footnote: In case you haven't heard, *Phantasmagoria* is Roberta's new adult horror game. With a 3-D rendered environment, live videotaped actors, and an ultra-spooky storyline, it's sure to make your hair stand on end and your skin crawl right off your bod!

Lorelei: What do you think is the hardest part of game design?

Roberta: Probably coming up with the proper interface. That's the hardest part. The stories aren't that tough to come up with.

Lorelei: That's the good part.

Roberta: Yup. I would say the toughest things to deal with are the interface and the technical aspects of how you want the game to work. I'm not a technical person by any means, but I have enough of an understanding to know what I can and can't do on the machine. I put lot of thought into that before I start working on a game. There's a certain visionary aspect to that. If you're thinking about a game to be released two years from now, you have to take into account what the technological advances will be.

Lorelei: Do you ever have ideas that are just beyond the ability of the computer to execute?

Roberta: All the time. That's one reason some of my games are ahead of their time. I like to push the envelope. My ideas are bigger than reality, for the most part. I always have to take it down a little bit. Of course, I'm in a unique position there. It helps to be a co-founder of Sierra, and to be married to the company's president, Ken Williams.

Lorelei: So you work with Ken during the design process when you're trying to figure out if you can actually do something on the computer?

Roberta: Oh yeah. A lot of people don't realize this, but Ken was a programmer before he was a president of a company, and he was actually an extremely good programmer. He's worked with compiler development, language development, artificial intelligence, lots of things. There are probably very few people in the computer industry that are better than Ken in the areas of programming and technology. It's just that he doesn't get much time to do that any more.

Lorelei: Do you think he misses it?

Roberta: I know he does. We talk about "One of those days when we're retired, what will we do?" I talk about maybe writing books, he talks about going back to programming. He really loves it. I'm very lucky I can talk to Ken about these ideas.

Lorelei: Are you planning on doing *King's Quest VIII*?

Roberta: (grins) That's what they tell me.

Lorelei: That's great. What do you see in the future for King's Quest?

Roberta: Boy. At this point in time, I already have two games in my head, and I really don't want to think about a third! The possibilities are endless.

Lorelei: It'll just have to be a surprise.

Roberta: Sure will! (laughs)

◆ ◆ ◆

So what was it like to work with Roberta? Well, it really wasn't bad, other than the occasional severe beatings she gave me, and the cattle prod she keeps in her desk. MADE YOU LOOK! I'm just kidding. It was terrific. Roberta is a delightful, creative and intelligent person. There's no such thing as impossible when you're working with her. She has a wonderfully infectious laugh, just like a little girl. Sometimes when we were jamming on ideas, coming up with every possible solution we could think of for a puzzle, we'd get really silly and just crack each other up. We'd be there with our heads on the table giggling wildly, and Ken would come in and roll his eyes at us and say "Don't you have WORK to do?" That would only make us giggle harder. Let me tell you a secret. That's where great ideas come from—fun. The more you laugh and open your eyes and enjoy the world, the more your mind will open and ideas will flow. Don't get me wrong. Designing *King's Quest VII* was hard work. Sometimes it was stay-up-all-night-and-drink-coffee-til-your-eyes-bug hard work. But it was always fun, because Roberta made it fun. When you play, I think you'll feel it.

Lorelei Shannon, King's Quest VII *co-designer.*

THE ART

Let's face it. This game is downright gorgeous. From the glowing hand-painted backgrounds to the hilarious animation, *King's Quest VII* rocks. It took a lot of work, imagination and creativity to get that way.

"The look of *King's Quest VII*," says Art Designer Andy Hoyos, "Is that of an intensely brilliant cartoon. It's different from anything we've done before in the series. We were inspired by the animated feature films of Disney and Don Bluth...particularly "Aladdin." The intensity of the palette used by the "Aladdin" artists was amazing."

Amazing is a good word for *King's Quest VII*'s nearly one hundred hand-painted backgrounds. Each one is a stunning work of art, created by some of the finest artists in the gaming industry. Once completed, each painting was scanned into the computer, retaining all of its sharpness and detail thanks to high resolution.

When asked what his favorite area of the game might be, Andy had to think hard. He (quite understandably) likes the entire game, and all of its different regions. After a while, he answered, "Probably the troll area. I'm not sure exactly why...Well, actually I think it's the characters in that region that I really like. As for backgrounds, I'd have to say Ooga Booga is my favorite. I guess I'm just drawn to creepiness (laughs).

Ooga Booga is a wonderful region of the game, but I suspect Andy's choice has been influenced by all the long hours he's spent art directing *Phantasmagoria* simultaneously with *King's Quest VII*. If that doesn't impress you, it should! An art director has an awesome responsibility to the project. "As Art Director," says Andy, "I'm responsible for the overall look of the project—the directions it takes aesthetically. I supervise the artistic end of the project, and make sure there's consistency between the animation and the backgrounds and everything. I have to break down the script into its individual constituent parts, analyze it, and figure out what art is needed. Keeping consistency throughout a game is very hard. But it's worth it. Coming up with the concepts for the environments is so much fun. Every time we do a new game, a whole new look is called for. I have such a lucky job. When I think about it, every aspect of what I do is so engrossing...even having to work on two projects simultaneously. The ability to switch gears and immerse myself in each project one after the other was a lot of fun."

I couldn't resist asking Andy if it was tiring. He just grinned at me and said, "What do you think?"

THE ANIMATION

You've never seen animation like this in a Sierra game before. In fact, you've probably never seen it in any other computer game before. It's feature-film quality animation, with characters that are lively, funny, and altogether unique. Lead animator Marc Hudgins had this to say about them: "The characters in *KQVII* run the gamut, from very 'straight' characters such as Rosella and Valanice, to the very cartooned types like the jackalope or the ghoul kids. For a character designer, they provided a great range of character types to develop. I really got to stretch myself as an artist designing all of these different character types."

Every piece of animation in the game is traditional paper animation, where each individual frame or "cel" of animation is drawn in pencil by an artist. Says Marc Hudgins: "The process is identical to the animation process used by feature films and

This is just a small portion of an animation sequence of a ghoul kid climbing up to his treehouse. This sequence actually took 40 individual drawings!

television. The only difference is that we scan the animation into the computer in its pencil phase, then color it digitally, then it is programmed into the game. The difference between game animation and traditional animation keeps getting more and more blurred. These days the traditional studios are using computers to scan and do their ink and paint just as we do. They even use computers instead of cameras to actually film the animation. On the other hand, we are beginning to incorporate more cinematic techniques into our games. It's kind of funny."

You'll see lots of funny things as you play this game. But fun has a price, and that's a lot of grueling work. For Marc Hudgins, coordinating a project this size was a Herculean task. "This was something new to all parties involved," he said. "To start with, the needs of this project were such that we used outside animation houses to help us. We had never gone outside our own art department for animation before. Second, most of the animation houses we were dealing with had little or no experience with making games. It was a bit of a challenge trying to communicate concepts unique to computer games, such as generic animation (animation that can happen anywhere) and the idea that three or four different actions could branch off of one animation. Just to make it a little more complex, some of the studios were in other parts of the world (St. Petersburg, Russia and Croatia), so we had language barriers to hurdle as well."

Despite the enormity of the task, Marc and the Sierra animators, with a little help from their friends around the world, created the most excellent animation in a computer game to date.

THE MUSIC

Whenever I tested *King's Quest VII* in my office at Sierra, the music and sound effects would always draw people in from the halls. Once they got in and saw the art and animation, it was all over. I had an audience for the rest of the afternoon. But I really can't blame them. The music of this game is pretty irresistible, thanks to musicians Jay Usher, Mark Seibert, and Neal Grandstaff. When asked about creating the music for a game this size, Jay had this to say: "With a game like *King's Quest VII* having over 70 distinctly different characters and moving through a myriad of completely different areas of play, it becomes quite a feat to keep the music for two separate heroines and the characters they meet transitioning smoothly at all times. I feel it's my responsibility to compose a musical score that creates the emotion to carry the player along through the game. The last time I counted, it looked like we were up to about 120 different tunes to accomplish this goal."

And where does the inspiration for this much music come from? Both Jay and Mark agree. "It comes from the characters themselves," says Mark. "I'm always bugging the artists to give me a copy of their pencil sketches," says Jay. "Just seeing how a character carries himself, acts, or walks ultimately determines the outcome of the music. We've tried to give each character his or her own 'mini-theme.' Each character is unique, so the music should be as well."

This game has music from beginning to end, just like a movie score. When the scene is scary, so is the music. When it's funny, the music is too. The hardware has finally caught up with the musician's ability to tell a musical story, to bring out the emotion of the action. "With the emergence of CD-ROM Multimedia computers," says Jay, "I finally feel that some of the limitations we've had to deal with in the past have been lifted and we're able to write what we hear in our hearts."

And all those sound effects! Every one had to be added into the game by the musicians, whether they looked them up in sound effect libraries, or created their own. Whenever I looked in on the sound studio, everybody seemed to be having way too much fun. Jay protests. "You don't realize how difficult it is to create a truly believable "raspberry" until you've had to record it yourself!"

THE PROGRAMMING

After all of this art, animation, music and sound is done, somebody has to pull it together. Those somebodies are the programmers. They are the people who weave the game together, making everything work in harmony as it should. This takes an enormous effort by a lot of people. Directing this effort are lead programmers Oliver Brelsford and Henry Yu. Oliver had this to say about his job: "I can't imagine what I'd rather be doing than taking beautiful paintings, wonderfully animated characters, music, voices and sound effects, and bringing them all to life in one seamless, interactive, cinematic experience. It's a thrill to think of the thousands of people who will enjoy what we've created."

Oliver makes it sound easy, but his job is a lot tougher than he lets on. The lead programmer must act as a liaison between programming and all of the other sub-teams, such as art and music. He also delegates programming tasks and schedules, synchronizing the flow of the workload to avoid bottlenecks. When you're dealing with a game this size, it's an astonishing feat. After all, King's Quest VII has at least five times as much animation as any other Sierra game ever created. Nope, that wasn't a misprint. Five times. No, really!

QUALITY ASSURANCE

Says Quality Assurance lead Dan Woolard: "QA is the last hurdle to be leapt before shipping. By walking the fine line between the designers' conception and the programmers' implementation, we often end up making neither happy, but all that comes with the territory. We're not content until the game looks good, sounds good, and plays good. The proof is the final version and, as always, the public lets us know how well we did the job."

So you think it would be fun to play games all day long? HAH! You see, part of the designer's job is testing the game for consistency. Roberta and I had to play the game until our eyes bugged out of our heads. I love Valanice with all my heart, but so help me, about the zillionth time she landed in the desert and asked for Rosella, I found my hand closing on a big, heavy edition of Roget's Thesaurus...But it was all worth it. That's what I keep telling myself anyway, as I sit in my lovely, clean, white cell and count my toes.

PULLING IT ALL TOGETHER:

THE PROJECT MANAGEMENT

Yes, there is somebody who has to oversee the entire production of an adventure game. Someone who has to make sure that all of the development teams—design, art, programming, music and QA—are working together to produce the best game possible. That person on *King's Quest VII* is our project manager, Mark Seibert. Mark not only coordinated the efforts of an enormous number of people, he did the scheduling, budgeting, tracking, and all the icky paperwork that every game requires and no one wants to do. If you had a question for him, he was there. In fact, he was ALWAYS there. I have a sneaking suspicion that he was living under his desk for a while. He put in more hours than anyone should ever have to. As he said, in his understated fashion:

"King's Quest VII was a real challenge from the beginning. I've enjoyed working on the King's Quest series since KQIV, as a musician; KQV as lead composer; KQVI, when I wrote "Girl in the Tower," and now producing the latest chapter in the saga, KQVII. The high resolution art and paper animation have made this, in my opinion, the most beautiful animated adventure yet. Take a look at the credits and consider the hundreds of people who worked on this project. It's been a real challenge trying to keep everyone going in the same direction."

I'll bet it was, too.

KING'S QUEST
Quest for the Crown

It was just a few days past Sir Graham's 19th birthday, but the young knight was bummed. Good King Edward was dying. Edward called for Graham, who was his favorite knight, and sent him on a dangerous mission. You see, many years back, the king had lost the three great treasures of Daventry: Merlin's Mirror, the Shield of Achilles, and the Chest of Gold. How'd he manage that, you ask? Well, between you and me, King Edward was a really sweet old guy, but a little naive. Anyway, ever since the magic treasures had been missing, the kingdom had gone into a tailspin. Edward sent Graham out to recover the lost treasures before the Kingdom of Daventry bit the dust, and promised to make the young knight king if he succeeded. Graham set out to look for the lost goodies, and found out in a big hurry what a mess Daventry had become. Under the influence of evil, it had filled up with witches, ogres, wicked sorcerers, and all sorts of unsavory critters. Graham was a smart kid, so he managed to whip them all, either by knocking the stuffing out of them, or outwitting them (ogres aren't the smartest guys around). He also made quite a few good buds, who helped him on his way. To make a long story short, he found the three treasures, and returned to the castle victorious. Graham was crowned king, but a few hours later, poor old Edward passed out of this veil of tears. That night, after his coronation, King Graham went into his chambers and cried, which goes to show you that it's OK for strong, brave dudes to show their feelings.

KING'S QUEST II
Romancing the Throne

Not too long after he took over the throne of Daventry, Graham realized that he was a lonely guy. Kings have a lot of responsibility, and it's hard for them to get out and meet girls. Graham was staring into the magic mirror one day, wondering if his biceps needed more work, when he saw a vision of the most beautiful lady in the world. This lovely babe was wasting away in a tower, so Graham wasted no time in setting out to find her. He packed his suntan lotion and headed for the tropical kingdom of Kolyma, searching for the three magic doors that would lead him to his lady's prison. Along the way, he met one of the magical, mysterious merfolk, who decided he was cool and introduced him to King Neptune. He entered the home of Hagatha, evil witch, lousy housekeeper, and kidnapper of Valanice (the woman of Graham's dreams), and he rescued a magical nightingale from right under her (pretty major) nose. He freed a winged horse from an evil spell which had turned it into a snake. Graham even met some dead guys, and if you've ever met any, you

know dead guys always have a really nasty attitude. He finally got to the Enchanted Isle, where Valanice was still locked up, wasting away from boredom and bad tower food. The tower was guarded by a humongous lion, which the good-hearted Graham managed to defeat without spilling a drop of its blood. So Graham freed Valanice, and she took one look at him and decided he had a really cute thing going on. She flipped for him. They were married immediately, and they're still crazy about each other to this day.

KING'S QUEST III
To Heir is Human

Talk about a bad break! King Graham and Queen Valanice produced the cutest pair of twins anybody'd ever seen. But when the baby boy was still just a squeaker, he was snatched from his home by the evil wizard Manannan, and made a slave. He was so little when the nasty sorcerer took him that he never even knew he was a prince. That creepy Manannan even changed the boy's name from Alexander to Gwydion. He made the poor kid clean his house, take care of his animals, cook for him, and basically do all his dirty work. He would punish poor Gwydion in a totally harsh manner for the smallest mistake, and sometimes for nothing at all. The one good thing Manannan did was to teach Gwydion to read. That was a big mistake, because knowledge really is power! Gwydion figured out that Manannan intended to kill him on his eighteenth birthday (some present!), and that was only a few weeks away. Gwydion dug through the wizard's books and found a righteous spell. He whipped up a cookie that turned the foul-tempered warlock into a foul-tempered alley cat. Gwydion hot-footed it down the mountain and got the heck out of there. After a dangerous adventure and a close encounter with some cranky pirates, Gwydion (he's really Alexander, though, remember?) jumped ship and swam to an unknown shore. What luck! He'd landed in Daventry! He didn't have much time to be jazzed about this, because a dragon was about to barbeque his long-lost twin sister Rosella. Using a big bad spell, Alexander clobbered the dragon. He was reunited with his family, and took his rightful place as crown prince. You can still make him look if you call him Gwydion, though.

KING'S QUEST IV
The Perils of Rosella

The royal family of Daventry just can't get a break. During the big party after Alexander's return, poor King Graham collapsed. Watching his daughter almost get turned into Dragon Flambé and then suddenly finding his long-lost son was just too much for his heart to handle. It looked like he was headed down that final road to Angelville, when a fairy queen named Genesta appeared to Rosella in the magic mirror. She told Rosella that there was this magic fruit in a land called Tamir which would save Graham's life. Genesta couldn't get it herself, because she'd been beaten up by the local evil fairy, Lolotte, who wanted to take over Tamir. Lolotte had swiped Genesta's magic talisman, which was a really powerful thing. With it, Lolotte could take over not just Tamir, but probably the rest of the world as well. This was not good, because evil fairies just don't make caring world leaders. Genesta whisked Rosella away to Tamir so she could get the fruit herself. After befriending seven dwarves, ditching a troll, and charming

a snake, Rosella found the fruit. Just then Lolotte sent some foul flying monkeys to snatch her up and carry her to the wicked fairy's castle. Rosella cleverly convinced Lolotte that she was just a peasant girl, which undoubtedly saved her bacon. Instead of killing her, Lolotte demanded that Rosella bring her three treasures which she hadn't been able to get for herself (bad fairies can't do everything, luckily). Rosella went out and got the three treasures, but when she got back, Lolotte laid a bombshell on her; she had decided to marry Rosella to her deformed son, Edgar. Rosella was mortified, but she soon found out that good looks aren't everything. Edgar, who was really a sweet guy, helped her escape from her room. Rosella crept into Lolotte's boudoir and shot her right through the heart with the golden arrow of Cupid. This caused the black-hearted fairy to have a love overload, and she dropped dead. Rosella took the talisman from her and headed back for Genesta's island. Using the talisman, Rosella fixed the severely sick Genesta right up. She also told the good fairy what a great guy Edgar was, so Genesta turned him into gorgeous young dude. Edgar had fallen hard for Rosella, and he asked her to marry him, but Rosella was just a kid and she wasn't ready for marriage. She let poor Edgar down easy, and went back to Daventry to save her dad. The family was finally all together again. For about five minutes.

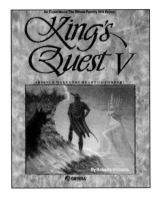

KING'S QUEST V
Absence Makes the Heart Go Yonder

Graham was out taking a stroll in the woods one day when his castle flew away. No, really. There was this big blast of evil magic, and the castle (with his whole family inside it) was gone. It just so happened that this owl named Cedric had seen the whole thing. He told Graham that Mordack, the brother of Manannan (remember him? Cat man?) had kidnapped his family in revenge for his brother's kittyfication. Cedric took Graham to a nice wizard named Crispinopher in the land of Serenia, who helped him prepare for his

trip to Mordack's island. Crispin gave Graham a bite of whitesnake to help him talk to animals, a battered magic wand, and Cedric, who whined about it, but finally agreed to go. Graham and Cedric stopped in at the capital of Serenia for supplies, and then headed off across the burning desert. They nearly croaked of thirst, sunburn, chapped lips and beaks. They managed to give some nasty bandits the slip, and finally got to the other side of the desert alive. They cut a deal with some savvy Gypsies, and then ventured into the Dark Forest. They met a wicked witch in the woods who would just as soon eat them as look at them, and they had to deal with a slippery little elf. Things got tougher from there. They kept going north, climbing up into some totally extreme and frozen mountains. The cold-hearted Queen Icebella captured them, but Graham managed to charm her, so she didn't feed him to her fearsome wolves. After meeting Bigfoot (no, really), Graham and Cedric got the heck out of the mountains. They found a boat on the shore of the ocean, and headed out to sea. The weather started getting rough, the tiny ship was tossed, and they ended up on an island full of man- and owl-eating harpies. They escaped by the skin of their teeth (I never understood that expression), but Cedric got the stuffing knocked out of him. He seemed to be winging his way to that great big birdcage in the sky. Graham packed him up anyway, got back into his boat, and kept sailing. They finally reached Mordack's castle. They snuck past the enchanted laser gates and wound their way through a labyrinth, looking for any trace of the royal family. Graham met the gorgeous princess Cassima, who had been enslaved by Mordack.

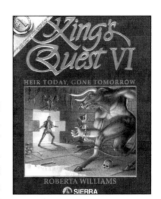

He promised to free her. She didn't believe him, because at that point, she didn't trust guys very much. Would you? Anyway, Graham found his family, and was he bummed. They had been shrunken down and stuck in a little glass bottle! Manannan the Kranky Kitty showed up to hassle him, but Graham bagged him. He recharged Crispin's wand in a bizarre cheese-powered machine, and got into an intense magical duel with Mordack. King Graham was doing really well for a guy who doesn't know beans about magic, but Mordack was about to whip him when Cedric managed to haul his pathetic self up and save Graham from a deadly blast of magic. Graham stomped Mordack once and for all, and his family was freed. So was Princess Cassima, who decided that all men aren't creeps after all. In fact, she decided Prince Alexander was kind of cute. She went back to her home in the Green Isles, and the royal family went back to Daventry and slept for a week. Cedric? Oh, he got over it. Owls have good immune systems.

◆ ◆ ◆

KING'S QUEST VI
Heir Today, Gone Tomorrow

The royal family of Daventry was finally all together. No one was kidnapped, no one had heart disease, and everyone was content. Okay, not everyone. Alexander was pining away for the lovely Cassima. He had taken one look at her and fallen madly in love. He was gazing into the magic mirror one day (doesn't that thing cause a lot of trouble?) and saw that poor Cassima had been locked up in a tower! He decided to sail out to the Green Isles and try to save her. His ship sailed for months, and finally one night it hit a terrible storm. The ship went down, and Alexander was separated from his crew. He started exploring the island where he'd been washed up, and found out that he had actually made it to the Green Isles, and had landed on the Isle of the Crown. He went to the castle to see Cassima, but he was told by the very sneaky-looking Vizier that she was engaged, and she didn't want to see him. Alexander didn't buy that one. Instead, he bought a magic map that allowed him to bop around between the various Green Isles in search of a way to save Cassima. He went to the Isle of Wonder, where he met a pack of punk gnomes and a bunch of talking veggies. He started to venture into Chess Land, but the silly sniping between the Red and White Queen was enough to make him want to keep

out of it. He went to the Isle of the Sacred Mountain, where he had to climb a brain-buster of a cliff. He solved all of the riddles, got the top, crawled into a cave, and found himself in a mind-boggling set of catacombs. I mean, these things were so bad, you could get lost just standing in one place. Cleverly avoiding the catacombs' tricks and traps, he got to the lair of a hideous Minotaur, who wanted to eat him for lunch. The Minotaur was basically a big bull at heart, and Alexander took care of him like any good toreador would. Alex finally got out of the catacombs, and was he glad to get some fresh air! He got to meet the lovely but snobbish Winged Ones, and an incredibly wise oracle. From there, he went to the mysterious Isle of the Mists, where the Druids hang out and do their Druid thing. So he kept on bouncing between the islands, bringing Beauty and her Beast together, befriending a down-in-the-mouth clown, and being followed around by a sneaky golden-eyed genie. Alexander even ventured into the Realm of the Dead, where all those dead guys with nasty attitudes originate. He got into it with the Lord of the Dead (yikes!) and won, saving the lives of Cassima's parents, the King and Queen of the Green Isles. All that was left to do was to save the princess herself. Alex snuck into the castle, managed to evade the fuzzy but fang-faced canine guards (imagine six-foot Scotty dogs with swords. Gives me the chills!), and burst in on the wedding of Cassima and the Vizier. There was a big hullabaloo, everybody was having a major cow—and Cassima turned into the genie! Okay, it wasn't really her. Cassima was never going to marry the Vizier. See, he just wanted to marry her so he could kill her and take over the throne, so he had the genie impersonate her— anyway. The upshot of all of this is, with Cassima's help, Alexander kicked the Vizier's pants, and the happy couple got married. Yay!

KING'S QUEST VII
The Princeless Bride

You think I'm giving you a plot summary before the hint section? HAH!

How This Book Works

The whole point of playing *King's Quest VII* is to explore its amazing regions for yourself, and to solve the many puzzles you will find there. However, some puzzles may be so well-hidden that you don't know where to begin. If this is your first experience with an adventure game, the whole thing may seem strange and baffling to you. If you feel you're really stuck at any point, look through this book until you find the question that best describes your problem.

Think of this book as your complete reference to *King's Quest VII*. The hint answers are arranged so that the first statement you read will usually be a subtle hint, and the last will be an outright solution. An answer with an asterisk (✤) beside it will be very specific, often giving you the exact actions to perform in order to solve the puzzle. We recommend you read only the hints you need and avoid reading the last answer of each question unless, of course, you're completely stumped. If you read every starred answer in this book, you'll complete the game very quickly, but you'll miss the challenge and excitement of exploring this marvelous world and solving its puzzles for yourself. For maximum adventuring pleasure, use this book with discretion!

SOME GENERAL ADVICE ABOUT THIS ADVENTURE GAME

✦ Read your documentation.

✦ Sierra adventure games open whole new worlds to you, and it's up to you to explore them. Walk around and explore by clicking the play cursor where you want to go.

✦ Move your cursor over the play screen. When the cursor highlights, that means you can click on that object and something will happen. What exactly will happen? That's for you to find out.

✦ I suggest that you try to interact with every character you meet every time you meet them, and always listen to what they have to say. It could be important!

✦ If the solution for a puzzle doesn't seem to be found in the region where you're currently playing, go back to the regions where you've been. You may think you've completed that region, but things can change while you're not looking.

✦ *King's Quest VII* is made up of chapters, and you can play the chapters in any order you wish. We suggest that you play it start to finish, so that you can experience the story as a whole. However, if you wish to play any chapter more than once, or out of order, just select that chapter when the Options screen comes up at the start of the game. When you do this, conditions will be different than if you played a continuous game—you will only have what you need for that chapter in your inventory, and optional things that could have

INVENTORY OBJECTS

✦ Sometimes when you click on an object on the screen, you will take it, and it will appear in your onscreen inventory.

✦ Once you have them, you can click inventory objects on other objects and characters on the screen. Pass your inventory item over the screen. If it highlights, you can use it there.

✦ You should inspect each inventory object carefully by clicking that object on the EYE next to the inventory window. Be sure to rotate it by dragging the cursor inside the inventory close-up window. Some inventory objects may hold secrets.

✦ You can sometimes combine inventory objects to create a third object by clicking one object on the other in the inventory window.

✦ You can sometimes "separate" an inventory object into two separate parts by clicking that object when it is in close-up view. Think creatively, and have fun!

AFTER YOU HAVE FINISHED *KING'S QUEST VII*

The last section of this hint book, entitled AFTER YOU'VE FINISHED THE GAME, contains a walk through, an object list, a list of things you may not have tried in the game, and some juicy gossip about the characters of *King's Quest VII*. If you've played all the way through and want to see what you may have missed, check it out. Warning! If you read this section before you've finished the game, you'll spoil it for yourself.

Thank you for buying *King's Quest VII*. A lot went into this game. A lot of time, effort, love, and heart. I hope you'll enjoy it as much as we enjoyed creating it for you. Write in and tell us what you thought!

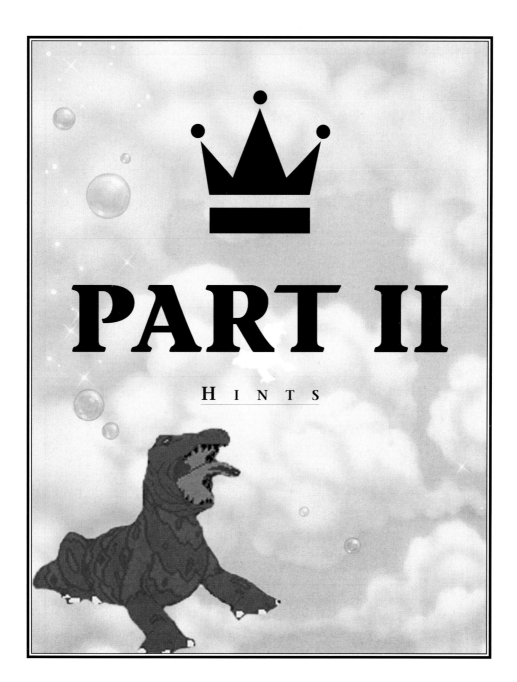

PART II

H I N T S

◆ ◆ ◆   GENERAL QUESTIONS   ◆ ◆ ◆

The music is too loud! The music is too soft!

❖ Click on the red jewel next to the inventory window to bring up the control panel. You can change the volume of the music by clicking on the arrows.

How can I save a game? How can I restore a game?

❖ Your documentation will tell you all.

I saw in the documentation that I can examine inventory objects up close. How exactly do I do that?

❖ Click on the object in your inventory. Click the object on the golden eye next to the inventory window. To rotate the object, click and drag your cursor in the direction you want the object to rotate. To exit the close-up, click on the square in the upper left hand corner of the close-up window.

I have to go to the dentist/meet with world leaders/get to school in half an hour, but I want to finish my chapter. How do I know how far I have to go?

❖ Click on the red jewel at the bottom of the screen to bring up the control panel. There is a chapter gauge on the panel that will tell you how far along you are.

This game is too hard!

❖ Nah. Make sure you click on anything and everything you can, and more than once! Listen carefully to every word the characters speak. Watch for all visual and musical clues. Almost everything you need to know to solve any puzzle will be given to you in the game.

What's with the button with the >> on it?

❖ That is a fast-forward button which will allow you to skip cartoons. We suggest you <u>do</u> <u>not</u> skip a cartoon until you have seen it at least once. You could miss something really important!

CHAPTER ONE

"Where in the blazes am I?"

What am I doing here? Why am I just standing in this desert?

❖ *You're just standing there because you have to click the play cursor to make your character walk. Explore the area! Click on anything that isn't nailed down! Move the cursor around the screen to find highlighted areas to click on.*

I've been wandering around the desert, but I can't leave! How do I get out of here?

✦ Ask the desert spirit. He knows.

✦ Look ahead. Stare the problem right in the mouth.

❖ *The way to leave the desert is through the mouth of the giant colossus head.*

Can I open the mouth of the colossus head?

✦ It's a two part question.

❖ *There are two turquoise keys which, when used together, can open the mouth of the great stone head.*

Where are the two turquoise keys?

✦ Find them yourself! You can discover that by playing the game.

❖ *Oh, all right. One is locked inside the altar in the stepped pyramid. The other is at the bottom of the pool of salt water. These will "unlock" the mouth of the colossus head.*

I knocked on the door of the "Rare Curiosities" shop, but the owner just keeps slamming the door in my face.

✦ He's slamming the door because he can't see you, and he doesn't know who you are.

✦ Maybe you should identify yourself so he won't be scared of you.

❖ *Click on the kangaroo rat to talk to him.*

The kangaroo rat told me that the jackalope took his glasses, but he still won't deal with me. Am I supposed to do something about it?

✦ Well, he didn't tell you just to make conversation.

✦ That jackalope is awfully irritating, isn't he? Maybe someone should slow him down.

❖ *You need to catch the jackalope.*

How can I possibly stop the jackalope? He's really fast.

✦ He sure is. He needs something that will trip him up.

✦ It really would be a blast to catch him, wouldn't it?

❖ *You can catch the jackalope by using the rope or the horn.*

Where do I get the rope?

✦ Someone has to give it to you.

❖ *The desert spirit can give you the rope. If you have the horn, however, he will never offer you the rope.*

Hints   27

Where do I get the horn?

✦ The answer is blowin' in the wind.

❖ *The horn can be found in the endless desert, next to the desert spirit's body. If you have the rope, the horn will not be there anymore. To get there, walk two screens south of the screen where you first entered the desert.*

Who is the desert spirit? Where can I find him?

✦ He's a wanderer of the outer desert.

✦ He's always on the move, so you have to be, too.

❖ *He's wandering around in the endless desert. Keep entering the endless desert screens until he appears.*

Every time I walk out into the endless desert, I die!

✦ So stop doing it already!

✦ You don't have to wander deep into the endless desert to find the desert spirit. He hangs around the edges.

❖ *You can't survive in the endless desert for very long. Never go more than a few screens into it. To be safe, map your progress through the desert on a sheet of graph paper. If you get lost, head north. You will eventually run into the cliff face. If you can remember whether you are east or west of the main playing area, you are saved!*

I drank the fresh water in the endless desert, but it didn't save me.

✦ The water will prolong your life, but it will not save you. It isn't meant for you.

❖ *The fresh water will do you the most good if you give it to someone else.*

I talked to the desert spirit, but he's not much help. He just keeps complaining about his thirst.

✦ That's a big fat hint, wouldn't you say?

❖ *Bring him some fresh water, and he'll do something for you.*

I don't have anything to carry water in.

✦ A pot would work well, don't you think?

❖ *There's a pot in the cave.*

I'm trying to take a pot, but they keep breaking.

✦ Not very persistent, are you?

❖ *Keep trying. You'll be able to take the last one.*

I gave the desert spirit some water, but he got really mad at me.

✦ That's because you gave him salt water. Geez!

✦ He wants fresh water.

❖ *What? You say there is no fresh water? Then you have to make some.*

How can I get fresh water?

✦ You have to create it with the water god at the well of salt water.

✦ The water god himself will tell you how.

❖ *The formula for creating fresh water is on the base of the water god statue.*

I found the formula for creating fresh water, but I don't understand it. What do I need to do?

✦ The first symbol represents salt water. That's what is in the pool now.

✦ The second symbol means that you have to cry into the water god's bowl.

✦ The third symbol means that you must place an ear of corn into the water god's hand.

❖ *If you do all that, the water god's bowl will fill with fresh water.*

Where do I get an ear of corn?

✦ There aren't any growing in the desert, so I guess you need to plant one.

❖ *Plant the corn kernel in the damp sand found along the cliff edge, next to the gourd plant.*

Where do I get a corn kernel?

✦ Try the cave. Remember, check out your inventory items carefully.

❖ *The corn kernel is inside the little woven basket. You have to open the basket lid in inventory and then rotate the basket to find it.*

How do I cry into the water god's bowl?

✦ You have to get into the character of Valanice. You're missing your daughter, right? That makes you very sad.

✦ Something of Rosella's will make Valanice cry.

❖ *Use Rosella's comb on the water god's bowl to make Valanice cry into the bowl. Note: For this to work, you must have looked at the inscription at the base of the water god statue.*

The desert spirit is offering me one of two items. Which should I take?

❖ I'm not going to tell you that! Just pick one! There is no wrong answer.

I just got a gift from the desert spirit, but now I don't know where the heck I am!

❖ *Don't panic. Just walk north and you'll find your way back to familiar territory.*

I have the rope. How do I use it to catch the jackalope?

✦ He seems to be a fellow of habit. He always follows a particular path.

✦ Notice how he always runs between those two cacti? Hmm.

❖ *Click the rope on one of the cacti to tie it across the path. Now stand back and watch the fun!*

I have the horn. How do I use it to catch the jackalope?

✦ Think of a jack-in-the-box.

✦ That jackalope thinks he's perfectly safe in his hole, doesn't he? He needs to be blasted out of his complacency!

❖ *Use the horn on one of the jackalope's holes. Heh heh heh!*

I gave the kangaroo rat back his glasses, and he wants to trade with me. What should I do?

✦ Offer him something.

❖ *Use one of your inventory objects on the kangaroo rat and see what happens.*

I keep offering things to the kangaroo rat, but he just wants to trade weird things that I don't want.

✦ Keep trying. Maybe he'll give you something good!

❖ *Try giving him a seed. A corn kernel is a seed, you know.*

The scorpion inside the stepped pyramid keeps killing me!

✦ Don't just stand there and let him get you, and DON'T click on him!

❖ *You either have to run from him (out the pyramid door), or get rid of him.*

How do I get rid of the scorpion?

✦ There are two ways to get rid of the scorpion. One way is easy, and involves a gift someone gave you. The other is harder. You have to be more resourceful to pull this one off.

✦ You can use the Big Bug Reducing Powder on the scorpion to get rid of him.

❖ *You can make the scorpion stick his tail in the wall by waving a flag at him.*

Where do I get Big Bug Reducing Powder?

❖ *The Desert Spirit can give it to you. However, if you chose the rope, you can never get the Big Bug Reducing Powder. You'll have to get rid of the scorpion another way.*

Where do I get a flag?

✦ You have to make the flag.

❖ *Make the flag by combining the stick with the ripped piece of petticoat in inventory.*

Where do I get the stick?

✦ It's just lying around. Just look for it.

❖ *The stick is next to the pool of salt water.*

Where do I get a ripped piece of petticoat?

✦ Oh, come on! You're just reading hints for the heck of it, aren't you?

❖ *The ripped piece of petticoat is still on the cactus that ripped it off your dress!*

Am I supposed to do something with this altar in the pyramid?

✦ It's a puzzle that you have to solve.

❖ *If you solve the altar puzzle, you will get one of the turquoise keys that will get you out of the desert.*

I made the scorpion stick his stinger in the wall and I'm trying to solve the altar puzzle, but the scorpion got loose and killed me.

❖ *Better solve faster. He's on a short timer.*

Nothing on the altar will move.

✦ Take a good look at it. It's all about rain, and crops, and green, growing things.

✦ Do you see a raindrop? How about an upside-down raindrop?

❖ *Click on the upside-down raindrop to release the colored stones.*

The colored stones on the altar came loose. What am I supposed to do with them?

✦ Have you tried taking them out and putting them other places on the altar?

✦ It's interesting how the beam of light travels right through the little statue's hands. If you were to put the colored stones in the statue's hands, it would create a beam of colored light, don't you think?

✦ What's the color of growing things?

❖ *Green! Put the blue stone and the yellow stone in the little statue's hands.*

What do I do with the red stone?

✦ Do you see something on the altar that could use some fiery color?

✦ What do plants need in order to grow, other than water?

❖ *Place the red gem on the sun carving on the altar. Here comes that key!*

What do I do with the purple stone?

✦ Take it into the cave and give it to the two-headed bear.

❖ *AHA! There is no purple stone! Caught you again!*

How do I get to the bottom of the pool of salt water? I can't possibly dive that deep.

✦ You're right, you can't.

❖ *It looks like you have to drain the pool.*

How do I drain the pool of salt water?

✦ The answer lies somewhere in the desert.

✦ On a cliff in the desert, to be more specific.

❖ *Click on the symbols on the cliff face next to the cave. They will tell you what to do.*

I don't understand the symbols on the cliff face near the cave.

✦ Just between you and me, the water god is kind of two-faced.

✦ That collar of his looks crooked, too.

✦ If the water god's bowl symbolizes water, maybe you need to make it symbolize a lack of water.

❖ *Click on the water god's face to turn his head around to the sun god face. Click on the sections of the water god's collar until the three turquoise stones line up just left of its chin. Click on the sun god's wristband to turn the bowl upside-down. There goes the water.*

Every time I try to take the key from the little statue's offering bowl, I drown!

✦ You have to leave something in the offering bowl in the place of the key.

✦ Something similar to what you're taking.

❖ *You must leave a turquoise object in the offering bowl before you can take the key.*

Where do I get a turquoise object?

✦ Maybe you should check out the local businesses.

❖ *You can get a turquoise object from the kangaroo rat.*

What can I trade to the kangaroo rat to get a turquoise object?

✦ He only trades for things that rhyme. You need a turquoise bead.

❖ *You need to give the kangaroo rat a seed in order to get the bead.*

Where do I get a seed?

✦ There are a couple of places to get a seed. You may already have one and not know it. How closely did you check the basket?

✦ Did you see anything growing in the desert that might have a seed? No, not the cacti!

❖ *There is a seed inside the split gourd. There's a corn kernel (yes, that's a seed) inside the basket.*

Uh-oh. I drained the pool of water, but now I think I want to give some fresh water to the desert spirit.

❖ *You can refill the pool by reconfiguring (clicking on) any moving part of the sun god statue. If you've already made fresh water and now you need some more, you can take another ear of corn and do the whole process over.*

I have both halves of the key, but I don't know what to do with them.

✦ You have to use them on the door that leads out of the desert.

✦ If you haven't figured it out yet, the colossus head is the door out of the desert. Look for something that could be a keyhole on the head.

❖ *The colossus head's lip plug is the keyhole.*

I can't get the pieces of the key to go into the keyhole.

✦ You can't put it into the keyhole in pieces.

❖ *Put the key together in inventory first.*

I have the two halves of the key, but they don't seem to fit together.

✦ Then you don't really have the two halves of the key.

❖ *Remember how there were two key-shaped turquoise objects in the offering bowl on the bottom of the well? You took the wrong one.*

I have a false key! How do I get the real one?

✦ The same way you got the false one. You have to trade for it.

❖ *Just place the false key in the little statue's offering bowl, and take out the real one. The sun god won't mind.*

Yes! I opened the door! But now a giant Gila monster wants to eat me, and the chapter's over!

❖ *That's called a cliffhanger, dear.*

CHAPTER TWO

"A troll is as a troll does."

What the heck is going on? Princess Rosella of Daventry can't be a TROLL!

✦ As the jackalope would say...

✦ Eee hee hee hee hee!

❖ *I guess you've got to find a way to turn her back into a human.*

I'm in the bedroom, and I'm a troll! How do I get out of here?

✦ Stop reading hints you don't need, you little troll, you!

❖ *Try the door! Sheesh!*

Whoa. I just got yelled at by a little old lady troll, and she gave me a list of things to go get so she can turn me back into a human. What should I do?

✦ Trust the nice troll lady.

❖ *Go find those ingredients!*

Oh, no! I can't remember everything in the list of ingredients!

❖ *Just click on Mathilde again. She'll tell you.*

Where do I get baked beetles?

✦ Sounds like a culinary delight to me!

❖ *Check the kitchen. They're in the bin on the counter.*

Every time I try to go into the kitchen, the cook throws me out. What should I do?

✦ Did you listen to what he was saying to his stew?

✦ There's something he'd really like to have for the final ingredient of his stew.

❖ *You need to distract the cook with a rat.*

Where do I get a rat?

✦ It would be pretty hard to catch a real rat. You should look for another kind of rat.

✦ How about a wind-up toy rat?

❖ *The bratty little troll girl left a toy rat behind in the great hall.*

Where do I get a gold bowl?

✦ Where do you keep the bowls at your house?

✦ No, I'm not talking to you guys who keep them in the linen closet.

❖ *Go look in the kitchen.*

I opened the stove, and the braised warthog with lemon sauce attacked me!

❖ *Did not. You're reading hints you don't need again!*

Where do I get a silver spoon?

✦ Not in the kitchen. Sorry!

✦ The spoon is somewhere else. It's a brand new spoon.

❖ *You can find a silver spoon in the metalsmithing area.*

I'm in the metalsmithing area, but I don't see any spoon.

❖ *Check in on the metalsmith from time to time. Sooner or later, he'll be casting a silver spoon in a mold.*

This incredibly obnoxious metal-smith won't let me do anything in here. How can I get rid of him?

✦ Remember the conversation between the two lady trolls in the mud bath?

✦ You need to knock him out with a lump of wet sulfur.

❖ *Throw the lump of wet sulfur into the forge. You can't do that until you've overheard the lady trolls' conversation though.*

Where do I get wet sulfur?

✦ Follow your nose. It always knows!

✦ Sulfur smells like rotten eggs.

❖ *There's a lump of wet sulfur embedded in the wall of the collapsed mine shaft.*

I tried to get the lump of wet sulfur, but I fell into that pit and died.

❖ *Be careful next time. There's one particular way to get across--just keep trying*

The metalsmith is out of the way, but the mold is too hot to touch.

✦ Man and Troll are tool-using creatures.

✦ Use the tongs on the mold to pick it up.

❖ *Use the tongs and mold on the bucket of water to cool it.*

Where do I get Water of Emerald?

✦ Seen any green, glowing water lately?

❖ *There are rock formation "pots" in the collapsed mine shaft area. One of them contains Water of Emerald.*

How do I take the Water of Emerald?

✦ A bowl would work.

❖ *Use the gold bowl to take the Water of Emerald.*

Where do I get a crystal dragon scale?

✦ From a crystal dragon.

❖ *There's a crystal dragon who lives beyond the stone bridge. You can get a scale from her.*

I can't get across the bridge because there's a big, nasty troll guarding it.

✦ There's nothing you can say to him or offer him that will get you across. You're going to have to fix his wagon!

❖ *Knock the troll off the bridge by fixing up the wagon and riding it down the hill.*

I tried to knock the troll off the bridge with the wagon, but it only has three wheels and it went right off the bridge.

✦ Looks like you need another wheel.

✦ There aren't any wheels lying around, so you're going to have to use something shaped like a wheel.

❖ *Fix the wagon using the round shield.*

Where do I get a shield?

✦ Oh, there's bound to be one hangin' around.

❖ *It's on the wall in the great hall, by the throne.*

I thought I fixed the wagon, but the wheel I used came flying off at the last minute and the wagon went off the bridge.

✦ You have to make sure the shield is fastened tightly to the wagon.

✦ You need something to use as a bolt to hold the shield onto the wagon.

✦ Remember, check all of your items carefully in inventory.

❖ *Remove the spike from the shield by clicking on it in inventory while "looking" at it in close-up mode. Use the spike on the shield as a fastener after you have put the shield on the wagon. That will keep the shield in place.*

I met the crystal dragon, but she's depressed and won't talk to me very much.

✦ Did you listen to what she said?

✦ There's something she badly needs. If she gets it, then she'll probably talk to you.

❖ *The dragon needs a spark. If you give her one, she'll talk to you.*

Where do I get a spark?

✦ From a fire.

✦ Seen any contained fires around here?

❖ *You can get a spark from the metalsmith's forge.*

I went to the forge, but there are no sparks in the fire.

✦ Did you watch the metalsmith while he was working?

✦ He did something to the fire to make it spark.

❖ *Click on the bellows to make the forge spark, or wait until he uses the bellows.*

I found the sparks, but I can't get them with my bare hands.

✦ You need something to put the spark in. Have you found anything that would naturally hold a little fire?

❖ *Use the lantern to catch the spark. It's in the collapsed mine shaft area.*

I gave the spark to the crystal dragon, but she just gave me a jewel and flew away!

✦ Oh, she's just really happy. She'll be back later.

❖ *Leave the room and come back and the dragon will be there.*

I came back to the crystal dragon's room, but she's sound asleep and I can't wake her up. How can I get one of her scales?

✦ She's not going to wake up. You can still get a scale, but you'll have to find a way to take it yourself.

✦ The dragon looks like a diamond, doesn't she? Use something that will cut diamonds.

❖ *Use the hammer and chisel on the crystal dragon's tail to get a scale.*

I keep getting squashed by the dragon's tail.

✦ Maybe you shouldn't stand under it then.

❖ *Wait until the tail is on the ground to get the scale.*

Where do I get a hammer and chisel?

✦ The jeweler can give you the hammer and chisel. Remember what he said about not being able to leave the Underground because he has no money?

✦ Give him something of great value.

❖ *Give the big gemstone to the jeweler and he will give you the hammer and chisel.*

Where do I get the big gemstone?

✦ Where did you see a lot of gems?

❖ *The crystal dragon will give it to you when you give her a spark.*

I think I have all of my ingredients. What do I do now?

❖ *Go talk to Mathilde.*

Mathilde said my gold bowl was really brass! How was I supposed to tell the difference?

✦ A princess should inspect her inventory items carefully!

❖ *Both of the bowls in the kitchen cupboard have stamps on the bottom. You need to go exchange the brass one for the gold one.*

But I had Water of Emerald in the brass bowl. Does that mean I have to get more?

❖ *'Fraid so - in your gold bowl.*

I got turned back into a human, but that nasty Malicia locked me in my room, and I can't get out.

✦ There's always a way out. Did you look around the room carefully?

✦ See anything unusual about the artwork?

❖ *There's a secret passage behind the portrait of the Troll King.*

How do I get up to the secret passage?

✦ I'm not going to furnish the answer to that right away.

✦ Let's table the question for now.

❖ *Make a ladder out of the furniture in the room. Do this by stacking the furniture below the portrait.*

My ladder is unstable and keeps falling over!

✦ A princess should know her physics.

✦ You put the biggest thing on the bottom, the medium thing in the middle, and the smallest thing on the top, right?

❖ *Put the nightstand on the bottom, the vanity chair in the middle, and the footstool on top. Climb away!*

I got out of the bedroom, but what should I do now?

✦ Seek a little help from your friends.

✦ You only have one friend in the Underground.

❖ *Talk to Mathilde.*

I tried to talk to Mathilde after escaping from my room, but she's all depressed and won't talk much.

✦ Poor thing. Maybe you should try to make her smile.

✦ Have you found anything that made you smile?

❖ *Use the Dragon Toad on Mathilde.*

Where do I get a Dragon Toad?

✦ You should know that! Ow!

❖ *You knocked it off the throne when you fell through the ventilation shaft. It's on the floor by the throne.*

I'm trying to get out of the Underground, but Malicia appeared in front of the door, and she blasted me.

✦ You'll never survive a face-to-face confrontation. You have to find a way to scare Malicia away from the door.

✦ You know what she's scared of. You heard her complaining about them earlier.

❖ *Use the wind-up rat on Malicia to scare her away.*

I made it to the elevator that goes to Ooga Booga. How do I fix it?

✦ You can't fix it until after you've been turned back into a human.

✦ Mathilde gave you a magic rope, right?

❖ *Use the magic rope on the bucket elevator.*

HELP! I went up in the elevator, but I think it's collapsing!

❖ *Hope you can hang on until chapter 4!*

◆ ◆ ◆ THE DESERT ◆ ◆ ◆

Yikes! This giant Gila monster ate me! What should I do?

✦ Pretend you're a cheese croquette and smile on the way down.

❖ *Don't like that idea? Well, you'd better turn around and run, then.*

I want to leave the desert, but how can I get past this Gila monster?

✦ He's awfully hungry. Maybe you should give him something other than yourself to eat.

✦ There's something around here that he likes. Have you seen any evidence of his messy eating habits lying around?

❖ *Give the Gila monster a prickly pear.*

Where do I get a prickly pear?

✦ Hmm. I wouldn't try a pomegranate tree.

❖ *From the prickly pear bush. It's near the giant stone head.*

I tried to take a prickly pear, but it's too prickly to touch.

✦ Use something to extend your reach.

❖ *Knock the prickly pear loose with the stick.*

Where do I get a stick?

✦ For the answer to that and other pressing questions...

❖ *Look at the chapter 1 hints.*

Do I need anything from the kangaroo rat in this chapter?

✦ Sure you do. There's something you should trade to him.

✦ You can try all your objects on the kangaroo rat, but don't read more into this hint than there really is.

❖ *Use the book on the kangaroo rat to get an object from him. He will give you a crook.*

◆ ◆ ◆   THE WOODS   ◆ ◆ ◆

I just met a talking stag in the woods! What should I do?

✦ He doesn't seem to be in the mood to play cards, does he?

❖ *Maybe you should talk to him for a while.*
Get all the information you can.

I tried to pull the stake out of the oak tree, but I couldn't.

✦ You can't. It's going to take someone supernatural to do that.

✦ The stag is pretty supernatural, isn't he?

❖ *He can't do it while he's a stag, though. You have to turn him back into his human shape.*

How can I turn the stag into his human shape?

✦ His curse is just a symptom of much worse things going on in the woods. When you find out how to save the woods, you'll find out how to transform the stag.

✦ There are two important things you must do to save the woods. They have to do with the giant statues by the river.

❖ *Ask the rock spirit. He will tell you what your two tasks are.*

Where can I find the rock spirit?

❖ *Look for the biggest rock in the forest.*

I found the rock spirit, but how do I wake him up?

✦ He certainly snores deeply, doesn't he. Look at that nose!

✦ Maybe if you tickled his nose, you could wake him up.

❖ *Tickle his nose with the feather. You must have talked to the stag about him before he will help you.*

Where do I get the object that will wake the rock spirit?

✦ You need a feather. Got any birds in your possession? How about fake birds?

✦ Remember, check your inventory items carefully.

❖ *There's a feather on the backside of the rubber chicken.*

Where do I get a rubber chicken?

✦ From a store specializing in fakes.

❖ *From the Faux Shop in the town of Falderal.*

I woke the rock spirit, but I didn't know what to ask him and he just got mad at me.

✦ You should ask someone in the woods about the rock spirit.

❖ *Talk to the stag and find out what to ask the rock spirit.*

I talked to the rock spirit. Where do I get sacred nectar?

✦ Follow your nose. It always knows.

✦ Sacred nectar smells just lovely. It's so sweet, it attracts hummingbirds.

❖ *The sacred nectar is in the flowers that grow on the cliff in the Maiden Statue area.*

I talked to the rock spirit. Where do I get sacred food?

✦ Guess what?

❖ *You can't in this chapter. Don't worry about it.*

I found the nectar, but how do I get it down from there?

✦ You're going to need some help.

✦ Do you know anyone who owes you a favor?

❖ *The hummingbird will get it for you after you've saved her from the spider.*

Where can I find a hummingbird?

✦ Stop reading hints and start exploring.

✦ The hummingbird is in the spider's web, on the far side of the river.

❖ *After you have saved her life, walk to the nectar flowers and click on them. She will come to you.*

I need something to put the nectar in. What can I use?

✦ Not your basket. It has holes in it.

❖ *How about your pot?*

I got the nectar. Now what do I do with it?

✦ You didn't talk to the rock spirit, did you?

✦ Go talk to the rock spirit. He'll tell you what to do.

❖ *Use the pot of nectar on the pitcher maiden's pitcher after you have talked to the rock spirit.*

I tried to cross the muddy river, but I fell in and died.

✦ There's only one place you can cross the river. Look for a likely spot.

❖ *You can cross the muddy river by clicking on the large stepping stones.*

I stuck my hand in the spider's web and got killed.

✦ Didn't your son tell you not to stick your hand in spider's webs?

❖ *That's not the way to save the hummingbird. Think of something else.*

How can I get rid of this creepy spider?

✦ No, don't try to use deadly force. That little beast needs some solitary confinement.

❖ *Put the spider in the basket.*

I got rid of the spider, but the hummingbird is still stuck.

✦ Oh, come on. You're just reading this for fun, right?

❖ *Click on her to pull her loose! Good grief!*

I turned the stag back into Attis, but the oak tree is still an oak tree.

❖ *There's nothing you can do to help her in this chapter.*

Every time I walk into the Wood of the Were Folk, I get eaten by a were-bear.

✦ Maybe you'd better stop going in there until you know more about it. Did you talk to the stag?

❖ *You can't go through the were-woods until you have the magic were-beast salve. You can get that in the town of Falderal.*

◆ ◆ ◆ THE TOWN OF FALDERAL ◆ ◆ ◆

This obnoxious little gate guard won't let me into the town.

✦ Did you look around before you read this?

✦ Sometimes it's best to just go around a problem.

❖ *Click on the little door to the right of the big gate. But be sure to talk to the gate guard. I wrote some great dialog for him.*

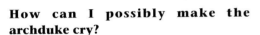

I got into Falderal, but this hyperactive poodle won't let me pass!

✦ Emotional little guy, isn't he?

✦ Perhaps you should appeal to his more sensitive side. It worked in "The Wizard of Oz."

❖ *You need to make the archduke cry.*

How can I possibly make the archduke cry?

✦ The same way you made yourself cry in the desert.

✦ Tell him the story of Rosella's disappearance.

❖ *Show him Rosella's golden comb.*

The stag told me that a merchant in Falderal might help me get through the were-woods. Who would that be?

✦ Only the slipperiest guy in town!

✦ Sssee anyone around here that fits that dessssscription?

❖ *It's the snake oil salesman in the central plaza.*

How do I ask the snake oil salesman for what I want?

✦ If you showed the comb to the stag in the woods, it won't be a problem.

✦ You want the salve so you can go search for Rosella, right? Tell him about Rosella.

❖ *If you didn't talk to the stag about Rosella, use Rosella's comb on the snake oil salesman to get to the heart of the matter.*

The snake oil salesman wants me to get him a magic statuette. Where do I find something like that?

✦ The snake oil salesman told you who has it.

❖ *It's in the archduke's office in the Town Hall.*

I can't get into the Town Hall because the badger guard keeps turning me away.

✦ He's turning you away because you're not dressed for the party. It's a masquerade party, get it?

❖ *You need a mask to get into Town Hall.*

Where do I get a mask?

✦ It's not in the Faux Shop. Ersatz is fresh out of masks.

✦ Try the other legitimate merchant in town.

❖ *The mask is in the china shop.*

I found a mask, but how can I get it?

✦ Maybe if you did something for the china shop owner, he'd be grateful and give you the mask.

✦ Talk to the china shop owner and find out what he wants most.

❖ *Bring Fernando his china bird back and he will give you the mask.*

Where do I find the china bird?

✦ Who in Falderal is dishonest and sneaky enough to steal a poor little bird?

❖ *That's right. The snake oil salesman has the bird.*

I found the china bird, but every time I try to save her, she screams and calls the snake oil salesman.

✦ Of course she screams. She doesn't know you. You must talk to her only friend first.

❖ *You have to talk to the china shop owner before trying to save the bird. He will tell you a phrase that will calm her.*

What's up with this mean mockingbird? All it does is insult me.

❖ *That's all it will ever do. It's a MOCKingbird.*

I got into the party in the Town Hall. How do I get into the rest of the building?

❖ *There's a doorway on the back wall. Click on the drapery to move it.*

Yikes! How can I find my way around these weird stairs?

❖ *Just explore them. They're not that hard to figure out.*

I got into the archduke's office, but I'm upside-down and I can't seem to do anything.

✦ You're right. You can't do anything upside-down.

❖ *You have to find a way to enter the archduke's study rightside-up.*

Oh no! I'm in the archduke's office upside-down and the magic statuette just fell on the ceiling! How can I get it?

✦ You can't get it from here.

❖ *You have to leave and come back into the archduke's office rightside-up.*

How can I enter the archduke's study rightside-up?

✦ Perhaps you should reflect on it.

✦ Remember Alice through the ———-———?

❖ *which one.*
The doorway is through one of the mirrors in the Powder Room. I'm not telling you

Where is the powder room?

❖ *It's one of the doors in the weird stairway. Just keep looking, and you'll find it.*

Okay, I give up. Where EXACTLY is the magic statuette?

✦ Did you check the desk?

❖ *It's in the archduke's desk drawer.*

I guess that chicken was right, because the moon just fell into the pond! What should I do?

❖ *Get it out, silly.*

How am I supposed to get the moon out of the pond?

✦ Ask Bo Peep. She might know.

✦ Ever hear the expression, "by hook or by ——-?"

❖ *You need to use the shepherd's crook on the pond to get the moon.*

Where do I get the shepherd's crook?

✦ There isn't one in all of Falderal. You have to go out of town to find one.

✦ The Kangaroo Rat in the desert has it. Give him something that rhymes with "crook".

❖ *You have to trade a book for the crook.*

Where do I get a book?

✦ You can find a book here in Falderal.

✦ It's in one of the local shops.

❖ *The book is found in the Faux Shop.*

How do I get into the Faux Shop?

✦ Don't believe everything you hear.

✦ Listen carefully to the archduke when you first meet him in chapter 3.

❖ *Eat the salt found at the well in the desert where the game started in Chapter 1.*

How do I get the book?

✦ Try asking the proprietor about it.

❖ *Click on the book to ask about it.*

Where do I get a wooden nickel?

✦ From under a bogus bird.

✦ Know any insulting egg-layers around here?

❖ *It's in the mockingbird's nest.*

How can I make the mockingbird move?

✦ Got a bazooka?

❖ *You can't. The mockingbird will fly away when it's darned good and ready to.*

Oh, no! I pulled the moon out of the pond, but the archduke just had me arrested!

✦ Nobody knows the trouble you've seen...

✦ I hope you like lifting weights and getting tattoos.

❖ *Don't worry. Your trial will take place in chapter 5.*

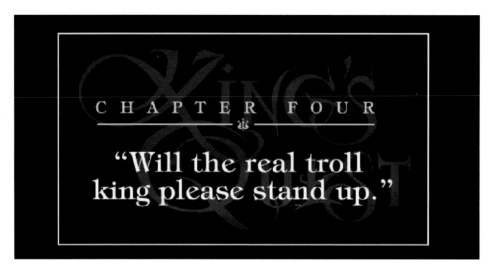

CHAPTER FOUR

"Will the real troll king please stand up."

◆ ◆ ◆   Ooga Booga Land   ◆ ◆ ◆

The elevator collapsed, and I died!

✦ You shouldn't have refused a helping hand. Or helping shovel, as the case may be.

❖ *When the gravedigger holds out his shovel to you, click on it.*

The gravedigger just saved my life, but he isn't saying anything.

❖ *So talk to him! Click on the nice man.*

The gravedigger told me somebody stole his rat. I'm supposed to find it, right?

❖ *You got it.*

This coroner seems to have a problem. What can I do to help him?

✦ Did you talk to him? Several times?

✦ He's got a little spinal integrity problem.

❖ *He's missing his backbone. He needs a new one.*

Where do I get a backbone?

◆ Did you look around? Did you look up?

❖ *The backbone is in the ghoul kids' treehouse.*

I went up into the ghoul kids' treehouse, but one of them was waiting for me and killed me.

❖ *There's nothing you can do about that. Sometimes there will be a ghoul kid in there, and sometimes not.*

I went up into the ghoul kids' treehouse, but they came climbing up the outside and caught me.

◆ You heard them coming, didn't you? You should have run.

◆ Dived is more like it.

❖ *If you hear them coming again, click on the window to leap out of it. You'll be all right. Really!*

I saw the ghoul kids playing with the gravedigger's rat, but they won't give it to me. How can I get it?

◆ They told you what they wanted for it, if you talked to them several times.

❖ *If you give them a weird pet, they will give you the rat.*

Where do I get a weird pet?

◆ There actually aren't too many around, but maybe someone could put one together for you.

◆ Who do you know in Ooga Booga land who has a lot of spare parts lying around?

❖ *The coroner will give you the weird pet if you give him his backbone.*

I got on the elevator to the ghoul kids' treehouse to give them the weird pet, but they killed me when I got there.

✦ Just look at those two. You shouldn't have trusted them.

❖ *Just put the weird pet on the elevator and send it up to the kids.*

The Boogeyman leaped out and killed me.

✦ Well, don't just stand there!

❖ *Run whenever the Boogeyman pops out. He doesn't want to exchange recipes with you, you know.*

The gravedigger offered to dig a hole for me. Where should it be?

✦ You're looking for someone in Ooga Booga land, remember?

❖ *You want the hole over the spot where the Troll King is imprisoned.*

The ghoul kids locked a cat in a coffin! How can I get it out?

✦ You'll need something to break the seal.

✦ Something strong enough to cut crystal.

❖ *Use your hammer and chisel on the cat's coffin.*

I blew the gravedigger's horn where I'm supposed to, but the Boogeyman popped up and got me. How the heck am I supposed to know when he's home?

✦ The ghoul kids can tell you.

✦ Remember their little chant?

❖ *Whenever the snake-shaped branch on the tree by the deadfall is pointing up, the Boogeyman is home. Whenever it's pointing down, the Boogeyman is out.*

Help! What's the combination to the lock on the Troll King's prison?

✦ It was painted all over Ooga Booga land.

✦ It was on the Manor House ruins and the gravedigger's "garage", remember?

❖ *The combination is Skull, Bat, Spider.*

I was trying to open the combination lock on the Troll King's prison, but the Boogeyman showed up and got me.

❖ *Better hurry next time.*

I got the Troll King's prison opened, but Malicia showed up and threw me in with him.

✦ Nothing you can do about that, my dear.

❖ *Ain't I a stinker?*

The Troll King and I got squished inside the Boogeyman's prison. How can I get out of here?

✦ First of all, you have to show something to the Troll King.

✦ Something that Mathilde said was his protector as a child, remember?

❖ *Show the dragon toad to the Troll King.*

The Troll King told me he needs to get the stone loose from his bracelet. How can I do that?

✦ With a tool you've used twice before.

✦ Come on, you got it from a jeweler!

❖ *Use the hammer and chisel on the Troll King's bracelet.*

I did everything I was supposed to do in the Troll King's prison, but we got squished anyway.

❖ *Do it faster!*

The Troll King and I escaped, but the boogeyman keeps getting me.

❖ *So, put on the veil already!*

How the heck am I supposed to get out of this place? The elevator collapsed, and the swamp monster keeps killing me.

✦ You have to get past the swamp monster, and you can't do it without help.

✦ Ask someone you know and trust in Ooga Booga to help you.

❖ *Get help from the Coroner.*

◆ ◆ ◆   IN THE SWAMP   ◆ ◆ ◆

The swamp monster gets me every time!

✦ Do you have the defoliant?

✦ No? See the question right above this one.

❖ *Yes? Then USE it on him!*

I tried to get the flower next to the carnivorous plant, but the plant ate me.

✦ You need something to distract the plant while you get the flower.

✦ Something tasty! Something with a little meat on it!

❖ *Use the foot in the bag on the carnivorous plant, and then quickly take the fragrant flower.*

Where do I get a foot in a bag?

✦ It was just lying around someplace...

❖ *You could have gotten the foot in a bag inside the ghoul kids' treehouse. If you've gone through the were-woods, you can't go back and get it now. Don't worry, you can find a different fragrant flower later.*

I need to get into Malicia's house, but I don't know how.

✦ The front door isn't going to work.

✦ Did you check around back?

❖ *There's a little hole under the tangle of roots at the back of the house.*

This hole is too small to crawl into.

✦ You're right. You need to enlarge it.

❖ *You need to use the shovel on the hole to enlarge it.*

Where do I get a shovel?

✦ Where did you last see a shovel?

❖ *It's leaning against the "garage" in the gravedigger's area. He threw it away.*

I crawled into Malicia's house, but she fried me before I even got to come up through the floorboards.

✦ You should have waited until she was not home to dig under her house.

✦ There's an easy way to tell if she's home or not. Aren't you afraid of that ferocious-sounding dog?

❖ *When she's home, the dog is barking.*

I got into Malicia's house and started to come up from the floorboards, but she came in and zapped me.

✦ Yep. It's usually a good idea to hide from evil people.

❖ *Click on the floorboards to duck back down.*

I ducked when Malicia came in, but her nasty little dog Cuddles smelled me and gave me away.

✦ You could always short-circuit his nose with something.

✦ You could use something that smells really bad, but is non-toxic to animals...

❖ *Use the defoliant on the little dog.*

The Troll King told me I'm looking for a special device in Malicia's house, but I can't find it!

✦ Malicia keeps it in a rather private place.

❖ *It's in her underwear drawer. The bottom in the chest of drawers.*

I was looking for the device, but Malicia came back in and fried me.

❖ *You took too long. Search quickly!*

I left Malicia's house, but for some reason, she showed up and zapped me.

✦ It's because you forgot something. Did you get what you came for? Did you clean up after yourself?

❖ *If you leave Malicia's house without the device, and/or if you don't put back all her underthings, take the stocking and shut the drawer, she'll get you.*

I left Malicia's house, and Malicia got me.

✦ Didn't you forget to do something?

❖ *Put your disguise back on!*

◆ ◆ ◆   THE WOODS   ◆ ◆ ◆

I'm trying to get through the were-woods, but the were-bear keeps getting me.

◆ Were-creatures just hate a certain type of metal, you know.

◆ Silver. They hate silver.

❖ *Your silver pellet can save you.*

I tried to get the were-bear with the silver pellet, but it didn't work, and he ate me anyway.

◆ You need to do something to really make that pellet fly.

◆ Use a sling to fling the pellet at the were-bear.

❖ *Combine the woolen stocking with the silver pellet in inventory. Now use it on the were-bear. Ouch!*

◆ ◆ ◆   IN FALDERAL   ◆ ◆ ◆

The Troll King thinks there may be a gate to the Underground in Falderal. How do I find it?

◆ Did you ask around? Talk to the locals and see what they say.

◆ It's somewhere in the Town Hall.

❖ *The entrance to the Underground is in the powder room.*

The mirror that leads to the archduke's office is boarded up.

❖ *It sure is. They didn't want any more of you bald-faced pink things getting in there.*

Hey! I'm locked in the powder room!

✦ Bummer. You'd better find another way out, then.

✦ Look around. There's bound to be a clue or two.

❖ *Check out the cherub statue.*

I think there's something written on the cherub statue, but I can't read it.

✦ That's because the plaque is tarnished.

✦ It needs to be polished with something coarse.

❖ *Use Malicia's rough wool stocking on the plaque to polish it.*

I read the verse on the cherub, but I don't understand it.

✦ The cherub wants fruit. Do you see any fruit in here?

✦ How about any golden fruit?

❖ *Use the golden grape on the cherub.*

Which golden grape?

❖ *The only one with a hot spot!*

How do I get the golden grape loose?

✦ With the most trusty tool in your inventory.

✦ That's right, you're going to use it for the fourth time!

❖ *Use your hammer and chisel.*

The doorway to the Underground is stuck partway open!

✦ You're not strong enough to push it open yourself. You need help.

❖ *Turn the Troll King into himself. He'll open it for you.*

How do I turn the Troll King back into himself?

✦ With the magic wand, remember?

❖ *Make sure the magic wand is set for trolls in inventory. Now use the magic wand on the scarab Troll King in inventory. If it is set for the device, it is set for trolls. If you see an "F," it is set for faeries. Click on the bottom of the wand to change the setting. Now use the magic wand on the scarab in inventory.*

◆ ◆ ◆   THE UNDERGROUND   ◆ ◆ ◆

Help! The real Troll King and the fake Troll King are in a terrible fight, and the lights just went out!

❖ Yikes! They're not coming back on until chapter 6!

Yikes! They're not coming back on until chapter 6!

CHAPTER FIVE

"Nightmare in Etheria."

◆ ◆ ◆ IN FALDERAL ◆ ◆ ◆

I can't get out of Falderal!

❖ *You sure can't. They won't let you out until you put the moon back into the sky.*

How do I get the moon back into the sky?

✦ You have to find a way to fling it there.

✦ Think slingshot.

✦ Think poultry.

❖ *Use the rubber chicken to fling the moon back into the sky.*

Where do I get a rubber chicken?

✦ Which store do you suppose is the most likely to carry a fake chicken?

❖ *That's right, the Faux Shop.*

I found the rubber chicken. How do I buy it?

✦ You have to trade for it.

✦ There's something the Faux Shop owner would really like. Something he ran out of earlier.

❖ *Use the mask on the Faux Shop owner to get the rubber chicken.*

I have the rubber chicken, but I don't know how to use it to get the moon back into the sky.

✦ Every slingshot has a big Y-shaped branch involved, right?

✦ There's a Y-shaped branch in Falderal. Just look for it.

❖ *Use the rubber chicken on the Y-shaped branch of the Mockingbird's tree. Use the moon on the chicken to fling it.*

The rubber chicken ran away!

✦ Can you blame him? How would you like it if someone used YOU as a slingshot?

❖ *Don't worry. He meets Chicken Petite, and they fall in love, get married, and raise hysterical babies that bounce off the walls. If you didn't get the feather from him earlier, then it will be left in the crook of the Y-shaped branch.*

◆ ◆ ◆   THE WOODS   ◆ ◆ ◆

The stag is still here. Should I talk to him?

❖ *YES!*

I want to know about the Rock Spirit, or sacred nectar, or starting the river of life. What should I do?

❖ *Check out these topics in the chapter 3 woods section, that's what!*

I have to talk to Ceres, but she's a tree. How do I change her back?

✦ Did you talk to Attis?

✦ There are two things wrong with the woods right now. If you fix the second problem, Ceres can be turned back into herself.

✦ The Rock Spirit will tell you what the problems are, and how to solve them.

❖ *You have to restart the cornucopia by placing sacred food into it.*

Where am I supposed to get sacred food?

❖ *You can get sacred food in Etheria.*

I have the sacred food. What do I do with it?

✦ The rock spirit TOLD you what to do with it!

❖ *Put it in the cornucopia maiden's horn of plenty.*

I started the cornucopia, but Ceres is still a tree.

✦ You have to do something to change her back.

✦ She needs an enchanted fruit. No, no, don't go to Tamir!

❖ *Give her the pomegranate.*

Where do I get the pomegranate?

✦ You just caused it to appear.

✦ It's right on top. You can't miss it.

❖ *It's in the cornucopia.*

How can I get through the were-woods without the were-bear eating me?

✦ You have a recipe for this, you know.

❖ *You have to use the were-beast salve you got from the snake-oil salesman.*

I used the salve on myself, but it didn't work.

✦ You forgot an important ingredient!

❖ *You have to combine the salve with the animal hair in inventory before you use it.*

I got the magic salve, but I'm supposed to use it with some animal hair. Where do I get animal hair?

✦ I suspect you scared a tuft of hair out of someone earlier. Go back and get it.

❖ *Use the tuft of hair the jackalope left behind when you scared him out of the kangaroo rat's glasses.*

Ceres told me I need a crystal shaft to capture a ray of sunlight. Where can I find one?

✦ Wicked fairies sometimes have good taste in lighting fixtures.

✦ It can be found in Malicia's house.

❖ *On the crystal lamp, silly!*

Where do I get the ray of pure sunlight?

✦ From the brightest place in Eldritch.

✦ Inside, not outside.

❖ *The ray of sunlight is in the stepped pyramid in the desert.*

I'm looking for a place to sleep. What should I do?

✦ Look somewhere other than the woods.

❖ *Try Ooga Booga.*

◆ ◆ ◆   IN THE SWAMP   ◆ ◆ ◆

That carnivorous plant ate me!

❖ *You should have stayed out of chomping range.*

I tried to go into Malicia's house, but the gargoyle got me.

✦ Don't use the front door then.

❖ *Go in the same way Rosella did. She dug the tunnel for you and everything!*

I went into Malicia's house, and she zapped me immediately!

✦ You shouldn't have gone in when she was home.

✦ If you're on your way into Ooga Booga land for the first time, you have no reason to go to Malicia's house.

❖ *You have to wait until her dog is not barking and she's not home before you go in.*

I poked my head up in Malicia's house, but she came back inside and zapped me.

✦ Duck!

❖ *Click on the floorboards to duck back down before she gets into the room.*

I hid under the floorboards when I heard Malicia coming, but her rotten little dog smelled me.

✦ You need to distract him with something.

✦ Dogs love to eat. Give him something really delicious.

❖ *Give the ambrosia to the dog.*

Where do I get ambrosia?

✦ Not in Ooga Booga land, Falderal, or the woods.

❖ *It's in Etheria.*

Where is the crystal shaft?

✦ You're just reading this hint for no reason. Admit it.

❖ *There are only about FIFTY of them on Malicia's lamp!*

I need a place to sleep.

❖ *Nobody sleeps in the swamp if they can help it! Go somewhere else.*

◆ ◆ ◆   IN OOGA BOOGA   ◆ ◆ ◆

The deadfall ate me!

❖ *Don't touch it, then!*

I saw a headless horseman riding through the sky. Can I do something with him?

✦ You sure can. Ask around.

❖ *Talk to the black dog about him.*

Yow! A big black dog jumped out of the shadows and won't stop barking at me.

✦ He's basically a nice dog. You just need to make friends with him.

✦ Give him something that dogs like.

❖ *Give the bone to the black dog.*

Where do I get a bone?

✦ Did you try the local bratty bone collectors?

❖ *It's in the ghoul kids' treehouse.*

I climbed up into the treehouse, and one of the kids was waiting for me and ambushed me!

❖ *There's nothing you can do about that. Going into their house is always a gamble. Try again!*

The ghoul kids climbed up and got me while I was in their house.

✦ Didn't you hear them coming? Jump for your life!

❖ *When you hear the ghoul kids coming, click on the window to jump out.*

I'm really tired of that Lady in Black killing me all the time. Can I get rid of her?

✦ She's really Count Tsepish's wife, you know. You should show her something that reminds her of her husband.

❖ *Use the medal on the Woman in Black.*

Where do I get a medal?

✦ That's a ruff question.

✦ You need to chew on that one for a while.

❖ *The black dog will give it to you. Talk to him as much as possible after giving him the bone.*

Where do I get the headless horseman's skull?

✦ It's right where he left it.

✦ His wife has been guarding it recently.

❖ *It's in the Count's tomb.*

I found the Count's tomb, but it's locked. How do I get in?

✦ It's a very explosive situation!

✦ Why don't you walk around and think about it for a while?

❖ *Use the firecracker on the keyhole to blow it open.*

Where do I get the firecracker?

✦ Who around here do you think has a firecracker?

✦ That's right, the local fiend patrol.

❖ *The ghoul kid will drop one in front of his treehouse at some point.*

The firecracker blew up and killed me.

❖ *That's what you get for standing there and holding it! Use it faster next time.*

I didn't find anything in the Count's tomb.

✦ Did you look around?

❖ *Click on the sarcophogus lid to open it. Click on it again to take the skull.*

How am I supposed to get the headless horseman to stop flying around?

✦ He's looking for something. You need to give it to him.

❖ *Give him his skull.*

How can I give the headless horseman his skull when he's flying around?

✦ He's not always flying around.

❖ *He touches down sometimes. You have to give it to him when he's riding on the ground.*

I tried to use the skull on the headless horseman, but he just ignored me.

✦ First of all, you have to use it on him when he's riding on the ground.

✦ Second, he won't notice you if you're off to the side.

❖ *Stand directly in the path of the headless horseman and use the skull on him.*

The headless horseman ran me down.

✦ You weren't quick enough on the draw.

❖ *Use his head on him faster next time.*

I'm looking for a place to sleep. What should I do?

✦ Ask your friends what you should do.

✦ You need a professional opinion.

❖ *Talk to the coroner. He'll help you.*

I'm in the coroner's house. How do I ask him to help me sleep?

✦ Did you talk to him?

✦ Did you look around? See anything that looks soft and comfy?

❖ *You have to click on him, and you have to click on the coffin.*

◆ ◆ ◆   IN ETHERIA   ◆ ◆ ◆

I just got dropped off in Etheria by Count Tsepish's horse. What should I do here?

✦ Start looking for help.

❖ *Walk around and explore.*

There are four rainbows here. How do I know which one goes where?

✦ Think of them in relation to the layout of the various lands below.

❖ *The upper right rainbow goes to Falderal. The upper left goes to the desert. The lower right goes to Ooga Booga to the woods. The lower left goes to the woods. It's almost logical!*

Ceres told me to look for the Three Fates. Where are they?

✦ They're hidden somewhere. Reflect on where they might be.

✦ They're aROUND here somewhere.

❖ *The Three Fates are in the gazing ball in the garden.*

How do I get into the gazing ball?

✦ It's a question of tone.

✦ Notice how the strings on the base of the ball look like a harp?

❖ *You have to play a particular melody on the strings to get into the ball.*

How do I find out what the musical key is?

✦ Did you hear anybody humming around here?

✦ Anybody small? Anybody that flies?

❖ *The dragonettes know the musical key.*

How do I find out what I need to know from the dragonettes?

✦ Your problem is they won't stay close to you for long enough. You need one to settle down for a while.

✦ They'd probably stop flying around if you fed them something, don't you think?

✦ Something really delicious?

❖ *Use ambrosia on the dragonettes. One will sing the musical key for you.*

I heard the musical key once, but I forgot it.

❖ *You can use ambrosia on the dragonettes as many times as you like, and they will play you the musical key every time.*

Where do I get ambrosia?

✦ The answer is blowin' in the wind.

✦ Climb the mountain for enlightenment and ambrosia.

❖ *The ambrosia is on the side of the Mountain of Winds, just above the plateau.*

I was trying to get ambrosia, but a big mean wind came along and ate me.

❖ *That happens. Just try again.*

I tried to go into the cave on the side of the Mountain of Winds, but a hideous monster popped out and got me.

✦ That's a nightmare monster. He'll never let you pass.

✦ You'll have to trap him.

❖ *Use the dream catcher on the nightmare monster.*

Where do I get the dream catcher?

✦ In a different plane of existence.

✦ Inside the circle.

❖ *The Three Fates will give it to you, but not until you've "dreamed" your way to Mab's island.*

The Fates told me I have to sleep to get to Mab's dream island. How can I sleep?

✦ That's a good question. You've got some pretty fierce insomnia by now.

✦ You can't sleep in Etheria. You have to look elsewhere.

❖ *Try Ooga Booga.*

I saw Mab, and she was frozen solid! What should I do?

✦ Talk to the wisest people you know.

❖ *Talk to the Three Fates, or Attis.*

The Three Fates told me to talk to someone about thawing Mab, but I'm not sure who they meant.

✦ There's only one Mother Nature in all the woods.

❖ *They mean Ceres.*

I found out how to thaw Mab, but I also have to get to Dreamland while awake. How can I do that?

✦ When it doubt, ask.

❖ *Ask the Three Fates. They'll tell you.*

Where can I find the Dream Weaver?

✦ Well, you can't miss his guard dog.

✦ The nightmare monster belongs to him.

❖ *He lives in the cave on the Mountain of Winds.*

I got past the nightmare monster, but the Dream Weaver is ignoring me.

✦ He's pretty spacey.

❖ *Click on him a couple of times. That'll get his attention. Now use the dream catcher on him.*

How do I use the Tapestry of Dreams?

❖ *Just use the tapestry on yourself.*

I'm supposed to catch Sirocco. Where can I find him?

✦ He looks like a horse, and he goes about 200 miles an hour.

❖ *He's the critter that zooms past the plateau on the Mountain of Winds. Not the one that eats you, now!*

How can I catch Sirocco? He keeps sweeping me off the mountain.

✦ Get out of his way.

❖ *Back up against the wall, next to the ambrosia, and use the magic bridle on Sirocco as he flies by.*

I got to the top of the Mountain of Winds, but Oberon and Titania just left me standing here.

❖ *Oh, no, and this was your last chapter. You'd better hope Rosella can take care of things.*

◆ ◆ ◆　IN DREAMLAND　◆ ◆ ◆

A horrible nightmare monster got me.

✦ The Dream Weaver told you something important about those guys. Remember?

✦ Nightmare monsters like to fight.

❖ *Use the dream catcher on the nightmare monster. Fight on the playground!*

Mab's still frozen in a block of ice. How do I free her?

✦ She just needs a little sunshine in her life.

❖ *Use the crystal shaft filled with sunlight on her.*

Where do I get the crystal shaft?

❖ *See the Woods section, above.*

Where do I get the sunlight?

❖ *See the Woods section, above.*

Oops. I came to Dreamland without the crystal shaft, or without charging it with sunlight. Am I in trouble?

❖ *No. The Tapestry of Dreams is waiting in your inventory.*

◆ ◆ ◆   THE DESERT   ◆ ◆ ◆

How do I get the sunlight?

✦ Just put it into something that can hold it.

❖ *Use the crystal shaft on the beam of sunlight in the stepped pyramid.*

Where do I get the crystal shaft?

❖ *See the Woods section, above.*

CHAPTER SIX

**"Ready, set...
BOOM!"**

Help! Both Troll Kings say the other one is the fake, and I'm supposed to turn him back into his real self. How can I tell who's who?

✦ It's all in the details.

✦ Use your ears and eyes.

❖ *The Troll Kings' voices are different. The real Troll King has purple eyes. The false Troll King has green eyes.*

How do I change the false Troll King into his real self?

✦ Use the magic wand given to you by the real Troll King.

✦ Be careful! Make sure you're using it correctly!

❖ *Look at the wand close-up in inventory. If there is a "T" on the ball, it is set for Trolls. If there is an "F", it is set for faeries. Set it for FAIRIES by clicking on the bottom of the handle. Use it on the false Troll King.*

Aaah! I'm trapped inside the cone of a volcano, and I'm about to get cooked!

✦ Better get the heck out of Dodge.

✦ Are you digging around for an answer?

❖ *Dig through the back wall.*

How do I dig through the back wall?

✦ You could use your hands, but...

❖ *You'd do a lot better by using the shovel.*

I was in the tunnels when a bunch of lava broke through and roasted me.

❖ *You have to hurry! In another few moments, the entire Realm of Eldritch could be roasted.*

I'm at the mechanical room door. How do I get in?

✦ Were you watching when the Troll King opened the door in chapter 4?

❖ *Click on the face in the following order: left eye, right eye, nose.*

I don't know how to stop the volcano!

✦ You can't stop the volcano.

❖ *The Troll King has to do it.*

The Troll King is knocked out. How do I revive him?

✦ Think all the way back to chapter 2. Remember the troll ladies in the mud bath? They told you how.

❖ *Use the fragrant flower on the Troll King.*

Where do I get a fragrant flower?

✦ You could have gotten one in the swamp, next to the carnivorous plant.

✦ You didn't? You'll have to find one here, then.

❖ *There's a fragrant flower growing through the grating by the mechanical room door.*

I see the fragrant flower, but I can't reach it.

✦ You need a stepping stone.

❖ *Use the stone that's embedded in the wall as a stepping stone.*

How can I get the stone loose from the wall?

✦ Your hammer and chisel won't cut it this time. You need the heavy equipment.

❖ *Use the shovel. Click on the stone to climb up.*

The Troll King stopped the volcano, but Malicia killed Edgar, and now she's coming for me!

✦ Better stop her.

✦ There's only one thing in the world that can stop her, and you have it.

❖ *Use the Mysterious Device you got from her house on Malicia.*

I used the device on Malicia, but nothing happened! Nothing at all!

✦ The Troll King told you something very important about that device.

✦ It has to be charged.

❖ *You didn't plug it in!*

Where am I supposed to plug in the device?

✦ Look around the mechanical room.

❖ *The plug is on the far left wall, across from the door.*

I used the device on Malicia, but it just made a little flash, and she zapped me anyway.

✦ You didn't let it charge long enough.

❖ *You have to plug in the device IMMEDIATELY after you re-enter the mechanical room, even before you wake the Troll King, or it won't be effective.*

Edgar's dead!!!

◆ Sheesh. What a depressing ending.

◆ No, wait! You happen to have something in your pocket...

❖ *Use the life given to you by the Black Cat on Edgar. Do it fast!*

Hey, I'm looking at an awesome cartoon. Is the game over?

❖ *'Fraid so. Congratulations! You finished King's Quest VIII!*

After You've Finished The Game

Did You Try...?

CHAPTER 1

+ Giving salt water to the desert spirit?

+ Catching the jackalope with the horn?

+ Catching the jackalope with the rope?

+ Using the bottle of powder on the scorpion?

+ Using the flag on the scorpion?

+ Using all of your inventory items on the kangaroo rat?

CHAPTER 2

+ Clicking on everything in the guest chamber?

+ Giving Mathilde the brass bowl?

+ Talking to the trolls in the mud bath?

+ Eating baked beetles three times?

+ Clicking on the metalsmith after you knock him out?

+ Using the spoon mold on the jeweler?

+ Walking past the bridge troll?

+ Riding the cart down the hill when it only has three wheels?

CHAPTER 3

+ Clicking on the spider?

+ Waking the rock spirit twice before talking to the stag?

+ Clicking on the muddy river three times?

+ Clicking on the flowing river three times?

+ Trying to take the China bird more than twice before talking to the bull?

+ Talking to the gatekeeper of Falderal?

- ✦ Clicking on everything in the Faux Shop?

- ✦ Clicking on the archduke at his party?

- ✦ Clicking on the archduk'es birthday cake?

- ✦ Using Rosella's comb on the magic statuette in inventory?

- ✦ Clicking on the Mockingbird over and over?

CHAPTER 4

- ✦ Clicking on the jack-in-the-box in the ghoul kids' treehouse?

- ✦ Getting on the elevator when the ghoul kids invite you to?

- ✦ Blowing the gravedigger's horn more than three times?

- ✦ Blowing the gravedigger's horn at the deadfall when the boogeyman's home?

- ✦ Chatting with the Coroner?

- ✦ Clicking on the Woman in Black?

- ✦ Clicking on the Woman in Black while wearing your veil?

- ✦ Turning the Troll King into himself while in Ooga Booga?

- ✦ Clicking on the ghoul kids while wearing your veil?

- ✦ Reading all of the gravestones?

- ✦ Clicking on the open grave?

- ✦ Walking on Mr. Crabby's grave?

- ✦ Knocking on Malicia's front door?

- ✦ Talking to the carnivorous plant?

- ✦ Clicking on the flowing river three times?

- ✦ Talking to the Falderal gate guard?

- ✦ Eating salt and going into the Faux shop?

- ✦ Talking to the people of Falderal?

CHAPTER 5

✦ Holding onto the firecracker instead of putting it into the keyhole of the tomb?

✦ Talking to the ghoul kids?

✦ Talking to the black cat?

✦ Using the Moon on Valanice?

✦ Chatting with the Coroner?

✦ Using the ear of corn on the cornucopia?

✦ Going back to all the lands and talking to the characters after going to Etheria?

CHAPTER 6

✦ Changing the real Troll King into a scarab during his fight with the false Troll King?

✦ Using the Mysterious Device on Malicia's little dog after using it on Malicia?

✦ Not using the black cat's life on Edgar?

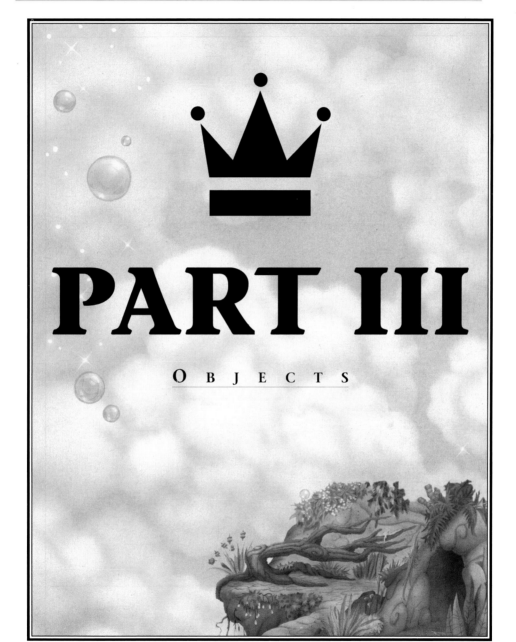

PART III

O B J E C T S

VALANICE

Rosella's Golden Comb

✦ In Valanice's possession at the start of the game (obtained during cartoon).

✦ Used to ask about Rosella throughout the game.

✦ Used on Valanice in the desert to make her cry (to get tears for making fresh water) in chapter 1.

✦ Used on the archduke in Falderal to get past him in chapter 3.

✦ Used on the magic statuette in inventory to find out information on Rosella in chapter 3 or 5.

Big Bug Reducing Powder

✦ Given to you by the desert spirit in chapter 1.

✦ Used in the stepped pyramid to defeat the giant scorpion in chapter 1.

The Rope

✦ Given to you by the desert spirit in chapter 1.

✦ Used to catch the jackalope in chapter 1.

NOTE: The above two items are mutually exclusive. The desert spirit will give you only one of them.

The Desert Spirit's Hunting Horn

✦ Found in the desert near the spirit's body in chapter 1.

✦ Can be used to catch the jackalope in chapter 1.

NOTE: The rope and the desert spirit's hunting horn are mutually exclusive. If you have one, you can't have the other.

Valanice's Piece of Ripped Petticoat

✦ As soon as Valanice starts walking in the desert in chapter 1, she rips her petticoat on a cactus. She can either pick up the ripped piece right then, or come back for it later.

✦ Used to bait the giant scorpion into sticking his stinger in the wall (inside stepped pyramid) in chapter 1.

The kangaroo rat's Glasses

✦ Found in the possession of the jackalope in chapter 1.

✦ Used on the kangaroo rat in chapter 1.

The Little Basket

✦ Found in the cave in the desert in chapter 1.

✦ Used to find the corn kernel in chapter 1.

✦ Used to catch the spider in chapter 3.

The Corn Kernel

✦ Found in the little basket when examined in inventory.

✦ Second corn kernel can be found in little basket when examined in inventory under special circumstances. See next notes.

✦ Used on the patch of damp sand to grow an ear of corn for the Water God in chapter 1.

✦ Can be used to trade with the kangaroo rat for the bead in chapter 1.

The Stick

✦ Found by the salt water pool in the desert in chapter 1.

✦ Used with Valanice's ripped petticoat to trick the giant scorpion into sticking his stinger in the wall in chapter 1.

✦ Used to get a prickly pear in chapter 1 or 3.

The Ear of Corn

✦ Grown from the planted corn kernel in the damp spot in the desert.

✦ Used on the hand of the statue of the Water God to get fresh water in chapter 1.

The First Puzzle Piece

✦ Found inside the stepped pyramid, inside the altar in the desert.

✦ Used in inventory with the other puzzle piece, then on the colossus head's lip plug to unlock it and escape the desert.

The Second Puzzle Piece

✦ Found on the bottom of the pool of salt water in the desert.

✦ Used in inventory on the other puzzle piece, then on the colossus head to escape the desert.

The Pot

✦ Found in the cave in the desert in chapter 1.

✦ Can be used to collect salt water to turn into fresh; used to carry fresh water in chapter 1.

✦ Used to get the nectar in chapter 3 or 5.

✦ Used (full of sacred nectar) on the pitcher maiden in chapter 3 or 5.

The Turquoise Bead

✦ Obtained from the kangaroo rat in trade in the desert in chapter 1.

✦ Exchanged for the second puzzle piece at the bottom of the pool of salt water in chapter 1.

The Gourd Seed

+ Found in the desert in a split gourd by the petroglyphs in chapter 1.

+ Used to trade with the kangaroo rat for the turquoise bead (seed for bead) in chapter 1.

The Turquoise Shape

+ Found at the bottom of the pool of salt water in the desert in chapter 1.

+ Can be used to trade for the real key at the bottom of the pool of salt water in chapter 1.

The Prickly Pear

+ Obtained from the prickly pear cactus in chapter 1 or 3.

+ Used in the colossus head tunnel to feed the Gila monster in chapter 3.

The China Bird

+ Found beside the snake oil salesman's wagon in chapter 3.

+ Given to the bull in the china shop in chapter 3.

The Mask

+ Found in the China Shop; given in exchange for the China Bird.

+ Used on Valanice as part of her disguise to get into the Town Hall in chapter 3.

+ Used on the Faux Shop owner to get the rubber chicken in chapter 3 or 5.

The Magic Statuette

+ Found in the archduke's office in chapter 3 .

+ Used with the comb in inventory to see Rosella in chapter 3 and 5.

+ Used to trade with the snake oil salesman for the were-salve in chapter 5.

The Wooden Nickel

- ✦ Found in the mockingbird's nest after the moon falls in chapter 3.
- ✦ Used on the Faux Shop owner to get the book in chapter 3.

The Book

- ✦ Received in exchange for the wooden nickel in the Faux Shop in chapter 3.
- ✦ Used to trade for a crook with the kangaroo rat in the desert in chapter 3.

The Crook

- ✦ Received from the kangaroo rat in exchange for the book in chapter 3.
- ✦ Used to get the moon out of the pond in chapter 3.

The Moon

- ✦ Found in the pond in Falderal in chapter 3.
- ✦ Used with the Rubber Chicken to fling it back into the sky in chapter 5.

The Rubber Chicken

- ✦ Obtained from the Faux Shop in exchange for the mask in chapter 3 or 5.
- ✦ Used on the Y-branch tree in Falderal to fling the moon in chapter 5.

The Were-beast Salve

- ✦ Given to you by the snake oil salesman in trade for the magic statuette in chapter 5.
- ✦ Used (with some animal hair) to get through the were-woods in chapter 5.

The Feather

- ✦ Found on the backside of the rubber chicken in inventory in chapter 3 or 5, or can be found on the Y-shaped branch after rubber chicken has run away. (if you didn't get it before).
- ✦ Used to awaken the Rock Spirit in the woods in chapter 3 or 5.

Sacred Nectar

+ Found on the cliff in the woods—obtained by the hummingbird in chapter 3 or 5.

+ Never used by itself. Used in the pot on the temple maiden to start the river flowing again in chapter 3 or 5.

The Jackalope Fur

+ Found in the desert on one of the two cacti or at the edge of the jackalope's hole, depending on where you caught him. Can be taken in chapters 1, 3 or 5.

+ Used with salve in inventory to turn into a were-jackalope and run through the were-woods in chapter 5.

The Femur Bone

+ Found in the ghoul kids' treehouse.

+ Used on the Black Dog to make friends with him in chapter 5.

The Horseman's Medal

+ Given to you by the Black Dog in chapter 5.

+ Used on the Woman in Black to get rid of her in chapter 5.

The Firecracker

+ Found near the kids' treehouse—dropped by a ghoul kid in chapter 5.

+ Used on the keyhole of the Headless Horseman's tomb to blow the door open in chapter 5.

The Horseman's Head

+ Found in the Horseman's tomb in chapter 5.

+ Used on the Headless Horseman to befriend him in chapter 5.

The Horseman's Fife

✦ Given to you by the Headless Horseman in chapter 5.

✦ Used to summon the ghost horse in chapter 5. (can't be used in Etheria).

Ambrosia

✦ Found on the plateau on the Mountain of Winds in chapter 5.

✦ Used to start the cornucopia in the woods in chapter 5.

✦ Used to feed to the rotten little dog in Malicia's house in Ooga Booga in chapter 5.

The Pomegranate

✦ Found in the cornucopia after you've started it in chapter 5.

✦ Used on the oak tree to turn her into Ceres in chapter 5.

The Crystal Shaft

✦ Found in Malicia's house in Ooga Booga in chapter 5.

✦ Used in the desert to collect a beam of light in chapter 5.

✦ Used in Mab's island in Dreamland to thaw her out in chapter 5.

The Dream Catcher

✦ Given to you by the Three Fates in chapter 5.

✦ Used to capture the nightmare outside the Dream Weaver's cave in chapter 5.

✦ Used to engage the Dreamland nightmare in combat in order to escape him (release one nightmare on another) in chapter 5.

The Tapestry of Dreams

✦ Given to you by the Dream Weaver in chapter 5.

✦ Used on Valanice to get to Mab's Island while awake in chapter 5.

The Magic Bridle

+ Given to you by Mab on her island in chapter 5.

+ Used to harness the wind Sirocco on the plateau on the Mountain of Winds in chapter 5.

ROSELLA

The Baked Beetles

+ Found in the Vulcanix Underground in the kitchen in chapter 2.

+ Given to Mathilde in chapter 2.

The Lantern

+ Found in the collapsed mine shaft area in chapter 2.

+ Used on the spark in the forge area to take it in chapter 2.

The Windup Rat

+ Found in the great hall in chapter 2.

+ Used it to distract the cook in chapter 2.

+ Used it to scare Malicie in chapter 2.

The Silver Spoon

+ Found in the forging area in chapter 2.

+ Given to Mathilde in chapter 2.

The Wet Sulfur

+ Found in the collapsed mine shaft area in chapter 2.

+ Used on the furnace in the forging room to knock out the forger in chapter 2.

The Gold Bowl

+ Found in a cupboard in the kitchen in chapter 2

+ Given to Mathilde in chapter 2.

The Brass Bowl

+ Found in a cupboard in the kitchen in chapter 2.

+ Has no use at all. Mathilde will throw it away and ask you to find a gold one in chapter 2.

The Round Shield

+ Found on the wall of the Great Hall in chapter 2.

+ Used with its spike to fix the cart and bowl over the bridge troll in chapter 2.

The Shield's Spike

+ Taken off of the round shield in inventory in chapter 2.

+ Used with the round shield to fix the cart and bowl over the bridge troll in chapter 2.

The Lantern with the Spark in It

+ Spark obtained in furnace of the forge in chapter 2.

+ Used on crystal dragon in chapter 2 to get big gem.

The Big Gem

+ Given to you by the dragon in exchange for the spark in chapter 2.

+ Used on the jeweler in the forging area to get his hammer and chisel in chapter 2.

The Hammer and Chisel

✦ Given to you by the jeweler in exchange for the big gem in chapter 2.

✦ Used to chisel off a crystal dragon scale in chapter 2.

✦ Used to open the cat coffin in Ooga Booga in chapter 4.

✦ Used to pry the gem out of the Troll King's bracelet in chapter 4.

✦ Used to get a golden grape in the powder room in Falderal in chapter 4.

The Crystal Dragon Scale

✦ Taken from the dragon by using the hammer and chisel in chapter 2.

✦ Given to Mathilde in chapter 2.

The Silver Pellet

✦ Used to be the silver spoon—melted while stirring the potion in chapter 2.

✦ Used with the woolen stocking to get through the were-woods in chapter 4.

The Dragon Toad Statue

✦ Found on the Troll King's throne in the Great Hall in chapter 2.

✦ Used to show Mathilde and get her to talk to you in chapter 2.

✦ Used on the Troll King to escape the coffin/closet in chapter 4.

The Enchanted Rope

✦ Given to you by Mathilde in chapter 2.

✦ Used to make the bucket elevator to Ooga Booga work in chapter 2.

The Backbone

✦ Found in the ghoul kids' treehouse in chapter 4.

✦ Used on the Coroner to fix his back in chapter 4.

The Weird Pet

- ✦ Given to Rosella by the coroner in exchange for the backbone in chapter 4.

✦ Given to the ghoul kids to get them to free the gravedigger's rat in chapter 4.

The Shrieking Horn

- ✦ Given to you by the gravedigger to summon him when you want him to dig in chapter 4.

✦ Used on Rosella by the deadfall when the Boogeyman's not home to call the gravedigger in chapter 4.

The Foot-In-A-Bag

- ✦ Found in the ghoul kids' treehouse in chapter 4.

- ✦ Used to get the Ooga Booga fragrant flower in chapter 4.

The Ooga Booga Fragrant Flower

- ✦ Found in the swamp next to a carnivorous plant in chapter 4.

- ✦ Used on the Troll King to awaken him in chapter 6.

The Extra Life

- ✦ Given to you by the black cat in chapter 4.

- ✦ Used to resurrect Edgar in chapter 6.

The Gravedigger's Rat

- ✦ Found at the ghoul kids' treehouse in chapter 4.

- ✦ Used on the gravedigger in chapter 4.

The Scarab Troll King

✦ He becomes an inventory object (a scarab beetle) in chapter 4.

✦ Used with the magic wand to turn him back into the Troll King in the powder room in chapter 4.

The Defoliant

✦ Given to you by the Coroner in chapter 4.

✦ Used to defeat the swamp monster in chapter 4.

✦ Used to zap Malicia's little dog in chapter 4.

The Shovel

✦ Found propped up against the gravedigger's "garage" in chapter 4.

✦ Used to dig into Malicia's house in chapter 4.

✦ Used to pry a stepping stone out of the tunnel wall in chapter 6.

The Woolen Stocking

✦ Found in Malicia's house in her dresser in chapter 4.

✦ Used with the silver pellet to make a sling and conk the were-bear in chapter 4.

✦ Used on the plaque to wipe away the tarnish in the powder room in chapter 4.

Mysterious Device

✦ Found in Malicia's house in her dresser in chapter 4.

Used on the plug in the mechanical room of the Underground to charge up in chapter 6.

✦ Used on Malicia in the Mechanical Room of the Underground in chapter 6 to turn her into a baby.

The Golden Grape (key to the Underground)

✦ Found on the column in the Powder Room of Falderal in chapter 6.

✦ Used on the cherub (keyhole) to open the passage to the Vulcanix Underground.

 The Troll King's Magic Wand

✦ Given to you by the Troll King in chapter 4.

✦ Used to change the Troll King back to himself in the Powder Room of Falderal in chapter 4.

✦ Used to change Edgar back to himself in the mechanical room in chapter 6.

 The Underground River Fragrant Flower

✦ Found in the Vulcanix Underground tunnel in chapter 6.

✦ Used to awaken the Troll King in chapter 6.

NOTE: The two fragrant flowers are mutually exclusive. If you have one, you can't get the other.

Chapter 1: Valanice

\<Watch sand cyclone cartoon. Rip petticoat.\>

✦ Take petticoat piece.

\<See jackalope chasing kangaroo rat cartoon.\>

\<Walk to the colossus head.\>

✦ Click on (and/or follow) footprints to Colossus head mouth.

\<Walk into the endless desert until you find the desert spirit.\>

✦ Click on the desert spirit to talk to him. Find out he needs water.

\<Walk to cave.\>

✦ Enter the cave.

✦ Take the little basket.

✦ Click on first three pots to get to good pot.

✦ Click on good pot to take it.

\<Walk to the pool of salt water.\>

✦ Click on sparkles to get salt.

✦ Click on Water God statue to admire it.

✦ Click on the base of the water god statue to read the inscription.

✦ Examine the little basket in inventory. Take off the lid and look inside. Rotate the basket in inventory.

✦ Use the play cursor to take the kernel of corn in the bottom of the basket.

\<Walk back to the cave entrance.\>

✦ Use the kernel of corn on the damp sand to plant it there.

<Watch corn grow.>

✦ Click on the new ear of corn to take it.

<Walk to the pool of salt water.>

✦ Use Rosella's comb on Valanice to make her cry.

<Walk up to the water god statue's bowl.>

✦ Use Rosella's comb on Water God's bowl to make Valanice cry into the water god's bowl (she will only cry into the bowl after you've looked at the pictogram on the base of the statue).

✦ Use the pot on the pool of salt water to get some salt water.

✦ Use the pot of salt water on the water god's bowl to dump it in.

✦ Use the ear of corn on the water god statue to place it in his hand.

<See water god cartoon.>

✦ Use pot on water god's bowl to take fresh water.

<Walk into the endless desert until you find the desert spirit.>

✦ Give the pot of fresh water to the desert spirit. He tells you about the colossus head being the way out of the desert.

<Follow the desert spirit to his body.>

✦ Choose the Big Bug Reducing Powder or the rope. Each has its advantages.

<Walk to the Stepped Pyramid. Confront the giant scorpion.>

✦ Use the Big Bug reducing powder on the scorpion to get rid of him OR...

✦ Use your petticoat piece on the stick (or vice-versa) in inventory. Use the flag on the giant scorpion to make him stick his stinger in the wall. BE CAREFUL! He won't stay stuck there forever.

<Approach the altar at the back of the temple.>

- ✦ Solve the puzzle on the altar:

- ✦ Click on the upside-down raindrop.

- ✦ Click on the red gem. Place it in the sun symbol.

- ✦ Click on the blue gem. Place it in the little idol's other hand.

- ✦ Click on the yellow gem. Place it in the little idol's hand.

<Watch the puzzle piece rise up from the altar.>

- ✦ Take the first key puzzle piece.

<Walk to the kangaroo rat's trading post.>

- ✦ Click on the door of the trading post to knock.

- ✦ Talk to the worried kangaroo rat. Learn that the jackalope has his glasses, and he won't do business until he has them back.

<If you have the rope, walk to the two cacti in the jackalope's path.>

- ✦ Click the rope on one of the two cacti to stretch it between them.

<See the jackalope get his horns caught. He drops the kangaroo rat's glasses. jackalope runs away, leaving a tuft of hair behind.>

- ✦ Take kangaroo rat's glasses.

- ✦ Take jackalope fur.

<OR...If you didn't get the rope from the desert spirit, walk to the dust storm area. Wait until the storm uncovers the desert spirit's horn.>

- ✦ Take the desert spirit's horn.

- ✦ Use the horn on yourself to blow through it and clear it.

<Walk to the jackalope's holes.>

- ✦ Use the horn on any of the jackalope's holes to blow horn down it.

<See jackalope pop up. He drops the kangaroo rat's glasses. The jackalope goes back into his hole, leaving a tuft of fur behind.>

✦ Take kangaroo rat's glasses.

✦ Take tuft of jackalope fur.

<After catching the jackalope either way, walk to the kangaroo rat's trading post.>

✦ Click on the kangaroo rat's door to knock.

✦ Use the kangaroo rat's glasses on him to give them back to him.

✦ Talk to the kangaroo rat. Use items on him to learn that he trades for things that rhyme.

<Walk to the cave entrance.>

✦ Click on the cracked gourd to get a seed.

<Walk back to the kangaroo rat.>

✦ Use the seed on the kangaroo rat, and get the bead.

<Walk to the water god statue at the pool of salt water.>

<NOTE: If you traded the corn (seed) for the bead, and you haven't got the fresh water yet, examine the inside of the little basket. You will find a second kernel of corn.>

✦ Click on the water god's face to turn it around to the sun god.

✦ Click on the three sections of the water god's collar until the three turquoise stones line up just left of the chin.

✦ Click on the statue's wristband (the one holding the bowl) to turn the bowl upside-down.

<Watch the pool of salt water drain.>

✦ Walk down the steps to the second idol in the bottom of the pool.

- ✦ Click on the idol to get a close-up.

- ✦ Click on the idol's bowl to make an observation.

- ✦ Use the turquoise bead on the idol's bowl to place it there.

- ✦ Take the second key puzzle piece from the idol's bowl.

<Climb up out of the empty pool.>

<Walk to the colossus head.>

- ✦ Put the two key puzzle pieces together in inventory.

- ✦ Use the two-part key on the colossus head's lip plug.

<Watch the colossus head's mouth open.>

<Walk into the colossus head's mouth. See Gila monster. End chapter 1.>

CHAPTER 2: ROSELLA

- ✦ Click on your door to open it.

<Walk to the Great Hall.>

<Be confronted by Mathilde.>

<See the bratty troll child cartoon.>

- ✦ Take the mechanical rat the child leaves behind.

- ✦ Click on Mathilde to talk to her.

- ✦ Hear ingredients list for potion that will make you human.

<Walk to the kitchen.>

<See kitchen cartoon.>

- ✦ Go into kitchen and look around. Get thrown out by cook.

<Walk back to kitchen.>

✦ Use mechanical rat on the chef to set it loose. Watch him chase it into the pantry.

✦ Take baked beetles from the bin on the counter of the kitchen.

✦ Click on one of the gold-colored bowls in the cupboard to take it.

✦ Examine the gold-colored bowl in inventory. Read the stamp on the bottom. If the stamp says "14k gold", keep the bowl. If the stamp says "brass—made in Falderal," use the bowl on the cupboard to put it down. Take the other bowl.

<Walk to the metalsmithing area.>

<See forger at work and creating sparks cartoon.>

✦ Talk to the jeweler. Learn of his dream to leave the Vulcanix Underground.

<Walk to the cave-in.>

✦ Click on the lantern half-buried in the wall to take it.

✦ Carefully jump across the pit of winds. Go all the way to the back.

✦ Click on the wet sulfur to take it.

✦ Click gold bowl on rock formation "pot" to get Water of Emerald.

<Walk to the great hall.>

<Walk to mud bath area.>

<Listen to what the troll women in the mud bath have to say.>

<Walk back to the metalsmithing area.>

✦ Use the wet sulfur on the forge.

<Watch the forger get silly and go to sleep.>

✦ Click on the tongs to get a cursor.

- Click the tongs cursor on the spoon mold to get a mold-and-tongs cursor.

- Use the mold-and-tongs cursor on the bucket of water to plunge it in and release the casting.

- Click on the bucket of water to reach in and take the silver spoon.

- Click on the bellows to make sparks flare in the forge.

- Click the lantern on the forge to catch a spark.

<Walk to the end of the mean troll's bridge.>

- Click on the troll to talk to him. He'll threaten you.

<Walk to the Great Hall.>

- Click on the round shield on the wall to take it.

<Walk back to the end of the bridge.>

- Examine the round shield in inventory. See the spike screwed into middle of shield.

- Unscrew the spike in inventory.

- Use the round shield on the three-wheeled cart to set it onto the axle as a wheel.

- Use the spike on the round shield to screw the shield into place.

- Click on the ride button.

<Watch the troll get knocked off the bridge.>

<Walk to the crystal dragon's cave.>

- Talk to the dragon to find out what's wrong with her.

- Click the lantern on the dragon to give her the spark.

- Take the big gem from the dragon.

<See the flight of the dragon.>

<Walk back to the forging area. Walk to the jeweler's room.>

✦ Use the big gem on the jeweler.

✦ Get the hammer and chisel from the jeweler.

<Walk to the crystal dragon's area.>

✦ Use the hammer and chisel on the sleeping dragon's tail while it's on the ground. Get the crystal scale.

<Walk back to the great hall.>

✦ Click on Mathilde to talk to her.

✦ Use gold bowl on Mathilde.

✦ Use each of your ingredients on the gold bowl or Mathilde.

<See Mathilde add a troll hair to the brew.>

<See Rosella drink the potion.>

<See Troll King and Malicia cartoon. Get zapped into your room.>

✦ Click on the portrait of the Troll King to get a close-up. Notice steam coming out of his nostrils.

✦ Click on nightstand to get a cursor. Move into position under the portrait.

✦ Click on vanity chair to get a cursor. Place on top of nightstand.

✦ Click on footstool to get a cursor. Place on top of vanity chair.

<Climb up and into the tunnel.>

<See Malicia and Troll King cartoon.>

<See Rosella slide down the wall of the Great Hall, knocking the dragon toad down as she falls.>

✦ Click on the dragon toad to take it.

- ✦ Click on the guest bedroom doorway.

<Overhear Malicia and Mathilde conversation.>

- ✦ Click on Mathilde to talk to her. Learn of some of her fears.

- ✦ Use the dragon toad on Mathilde to show it to her.

<See Mathilde asking the toad about the Troll King's whereabouts. Learn that he is being held in Ooga Booga.>

- ✦ Get magic rope from Mathilde.

<Walk toward the gate.>

<See Malicia appear and threaten Rosella.>

- ✦ Use mechanical rat on Malicia to scare her away.

<Walk through to the bucket elevator in the troll bridge screen.>

- ✦ Click the magic rope on the elevator to fix it.

- ✦ Click on the bucket elevator to get in.

- ✦ Click on the rope to pull yourself up.

<Hear the elevator shaft start to collapse. End chapter 2.>

CHAPTER 3: VALANICE

<See the Gila monster confronting Valanice cartoon.>

<Turn around, run out of the tunnel and back out into the desert.>

- ✦ Use the stick on the prickly pear bush to knock it loose.

- ✦ Take the prickly pear.

<Walk back into the tunnel.>

◆ Use the prickly pear on the Gila monster.

<See the Gila monster go away.>

<Walk through the tunnel to the woods.>

<Walk to the oak tree.>

◆ Click on the stag to talk to him.

◆ Use Rosella's comb on the stag to tell him your story. Get information about getting through the were-woods.

<Walk to the rapids in the muddy river.>

◆ Carefully cross the river stepping on the stones.

<See the hummingbird calling for help in the spider's web.>

◆ Use the basket on the spider to capture him.

◆ Click on the hummingbird to rescue her from the web.

<Proceed through to Falderal.>

<See the gate keeper's outrageous demand.>

◆ Click on the small door to open it.

<Walk through into town.>

<Watch archduke confronting Valanice cartoon.>

◆ Use Rosella's comb on the archduke to tell him your story and gain his sympathy.

<Walk over to the snake oil salesman's wagon.>

◆ Click cursor or comb on the snake oil salesman to talk to him. Ask about the were-beast salve. Learn he wants the archduke's magic statuette in exchange for it.

<Walk to the front doors of Town Hall.>

◆ Click on the sign on the door to read it. Find out about the masquerade ball.

<Walk to the China Shop.>

◆ Talk to the bull. Learn that he has lost his friend, the china bird.

<Walk back to the snake oil salesman's wagon.>

◆ Click to uncover the china bird's cage.

◆ Click on china bird cage door to open it.

◆ Click on the china bird to reassure her. She goes into your inventory.

<Walk back to the China Shop.>

◆ Give the china bird to the China Shop owner. Get the mask in return.

<Walk to the front doors of the Town Hall.>

◆ Use the mask on Valanice.

◆ Click on town hall door to knock.

<Walk into the town hall. See Duke's birthday cartoon.>

◆ Click on tapestry on back wall to enter stairway.

<Put mask back into inventory.>

<Wander around the stairs until you find the entrance to the powder room (rightside-up door).>

◆ Click on the powder room. Get smacked in the face with powder.

◆ Click on the powder room again to enter.

◆ Click on the third mirror from the right (upside-down Valanice mirror) to go through it into the archduke's study.

◆ Click on the archduke's desk drawer to open it.

- ✦ Click on the statuette in the drawer to take it.
- ✦ Use Rosella's comb on the magic statuette in inventory.

<See vision of Rosella coming up the bucket elevator into Ooga Booga.>

<Leave the study.>

<Exit the Town Hall.>

<Go east to the Central Plaza.>

<See the moon fall into the pool cartoon. See the mockingbird fly away.>

- ✦ Click on the mockingbird's nest to get the wooden nickel.
- ✦ Use salt on Valanice.

<Walk to the Faux Shop.>

- ✦ Use wooden nickel on Faux Shop owner to get a book.
- ✦ Use mask on Faux Shop owner to get the rubber chicken.
- ✦ Inspect the rubber chicken in inventory. Find and click on the feather.

<Walk back to the woods.>

- ✦ Click the feather on the Rock Spirit to awaken him. Learn how to start the pitcher and cornucopia.

<Walk to the nectar plants.>

- ✦ Click on the nectar plants. The hummingbird flies up to help.
- ✦ Use pot on nectar plants to catch nectar in pot.

<Walk to the pitcher maiden.>

- ✦ Use pot of nectar on pitcher maiden's pitcher.

<See water of life start to flow. See Attis turned into himself cartoon. See Attis pull stake out of oak tree cartoon.>

NOTE: Starting the river of life can be done in chapter 5 instead of 3, if you want.

<Walk to the desert.>

✦ Click on the kangaroo rat's door to knock.

✦ Click the book on the kangaroo rat. Get the crook.

<Walk back to Falderal. Approach the pool.>

✦ Click crook on the moon in the pool to take it.

<Drop the crook into the pond. See Valanice arrested cartoon. End chapter 3.>

CHAPTER 4: ROSELLA

<See the shovel held out to you.>

✦ Click on the shovel to get rescued by the gravedigger.

<See the gravedigger go back to work, complaining to himself.>

✦ Click on the gravedigger to talk to him. Get measured for a grave.

✦ Click on the gravedigger again to talk to him. Learn about his machine, and the rat stolen by the ghoul kids.

✦ Click on the graffiti on the tomb doors to get a good look at it.

✦ Run from the boogeyman every time you see him.

<Walk to the Coroner's house.>

✦ Click on the Coroner's door to knock.

✦ Click on the Coroner to talk to him when he answers the door.

\<Learn that the Coroner needs a backbone.\>

\<Leave the Coroner's house. Walk to the Ghoul Kids' treehouse.\>

\<Look to see if the elevator is up or down. If the elevator is down, you can enter. If it is up, leave and come back until it is down.\>

✦ Click on the elevator to enter the ghoul kids' treehouse.

✦ Click on the backbone to take it.

✦ Click on the foot in a bag to take it.

✦ Click on the elevator to go back down from the ghoul kids' treehouse.

\<Walk back to the Coroner's house.\>

✦ Click on the Coroner's door to knock.

✦ Use the backbone on the Coroner when he answers the door.

\<See Coroner swallow the backbone. The Coroner gives you a weird pet in a box.\>

\<Leave the Coroner's house and walk to the ghoul kids' treehouse.\>

\<Listen to ghoul kids' nursery rhyme. It tells you how to determine if the boogeyman is home or not.\>

✦ Talk to the ghoul kids. Get hint about wanting a better pet.

✦ Use the weird pet in a box on the platform elevator to give it to the ghoul kids.

\<See treehouse shaking cartoon.\>

\<Catch the rat when he jumps from the treehouse.\>

\<Walk back to the gravedigger.\>

✦ Use the rat on the gravedigger to give it to him.

\<The gravedigger is grateful, and offers to dig a hole for you wherever you want. Get horn to summon gravedigger.\>

\<Walk to the ghoul kids' treehouse. See ghoul kids with cat in coffin. Ghoul kids run off.\>

✦ Use hammer and chisel on coffin to free cat.

\<The cat tells you that the Troll King is imprisoned beneath the deadfall. Get a life from her.\>

\<Walk to the deadfall.\>

\<Look at the deadfall. Make sure the Boogeyman isn't home. When he's home, the snake-shaped stick points up. When he's not, the snake-shaped stick points down.\>

✦ Use the horn on Rosella to call the gravedigger.

\<See the gravedigger dig down into the ground beneath the deadfall for you. The gravedigger leaves.\>

✦ Click on the gravedigger's tunnel to go down under the deadfall.

✦ Click on the combination lock on the chains around the coffin/closet to get a close-up.

✦ Click on the combination lock to turn the dial and open it. (The combination is skull, bat, spider.)

\<Barely have time to meet the Troll King before Malicia shows up. See Rosella and Troll King magically imprisoned in the closet/coffin.\>

\<See brief cartoon where Rosella and Troll King introduce themselves. Skeletons start banging on coffin.\>

✦ Use dragon toad on the Troll King.

\<Troll King shows you the jewel in his bracelet.\>

✦ Use the hammer and chisel on the Troll King's jewel to pry it loose.

<See the Troll King put the jewel in the toad's head. Watch the toad dig a tunnel for you. Leave the tunnel and emerge into the cemetary area. See brief info cartoon. See Troll King turn himself into a scarab. Get scarab and magic wand of transformation. See Troll King create a veil for you>

✦ Click on the veil to take it.

✦ Use veil on Rosella to disguise her.

<Walk to the Coroner's house.>

✦ Click on the Coroner's door to knock.

<Get pulled inside by the Coroner. Learn that Malicia is looking for you.>

✦ Click on the Coroner to tell him that you have to leave through the swamp.

<See Coroner rummage around in his cupboards. Get defoliant.>

<Leave the Coroner's house. Walk to the gate that leads out to the swamp.>

✦ Click on the gate to open it.

<See the swamp monster confront Rosella.>

✦ Use the defoliant on the swamp monster.

<See the swamp monster crumble away.>

<Walk through the swamp to Malicia's house>.

✦ Click on the tangle of roots behind Malicia's house to remove them.

✦ Click on the small hole under the roots to examine it.

<Walk back into Ooga Booga. Walk to the gravedigger's area.>

✦ Click on the shovel to take it.

<Walk back out through the gate into the swamp. Walk to the back of Malicia's house. Make sure the dog is not barking.>

✦ Use the shovel on the small hole to enlarge it.

✦ Click on the tunnel to crawl in.

<Rosella takes off the veil before she crawls in.>

<See cartoon of Rosella's head poking up through the floorboards. Hear Malicia coming.>

✦ Click on floorboards to duck back down.

<See through knothole. Little dog starts sniffing you.>

✦ Use defoliant on little dog's nose.

<See little dog sneeze and snort. Malicia carries him out of the room.>

✦ Click on the knothole to push up the board.

✦ Click on the room to climb up out of the floorboards.

✦ Click on the bottom drawer of Malicia's dresser to open it.

✦ Click on the drawer to pull out underwear item and woolen stocking.

✦ Click on the drawer to pull out the Mysterious Device. It goes into inventory.

✦ Click on the three underwear items to put them back in the drawer.

✦ Click on the woolen stocking to take it.

✦ Click on the drawer to close it.

✦ Click on the floorboards to crawl back down into the tunnel.

<See Rosella emerge from the tunnel.>

✦ Click on the veil to take it.

✦ Use the veil on Rosella to put on the disguise again.

✦ Walk to the carnivorous plant. STOP SHORT of the carnivorous plant or he will eat you.

✦ Use the foot in the bag on the carnivorous plant.

✦ While the carnivorous plant is chomping, click on the fragrant flower to take it.

<Continue on through the swamp.>

<Enter the were-woods. Get confronted by the were-bear.>

✦ Use the woolen stocking on the silver pellet in inventory.

✦ Use the woolen stocking with silver pellet on the were-bear to bonk him in the nose.

<Run through the were-woods. Get veil snatched off by were-bear. Emerge into the regular woods.>

<Go through into Falderal.>

<Walk to the Town Hall.>

✦ Click on the door to go in.

<Walk through the assembly room.>

✦ Click on the tapestry to go into the stairway.

<Find your way to the powder room.>

✦ Click on the powder room door. Get smacked in the face with the powder puff.

✦ Click on door again to enter.

✦ Use woolen stocking on base of cherub to clean it.

✦ Click on base of cherub to read instructions.

✦ Use hammer and chisel on the loose grape on the fountain to take it.

✦ Use loose grape on cherub's mouth.

\<See cherub spitting/fountain opening cartoon. See fountain stick partway open.\>

✦ Use magic wand of transformation on the scarab in inventory to turn the Troll King into himself.

\<See Troll King open fountain the rest of the way.\>

✦ Click on the fountain to climb in.

\<Fall through into the Vulcanix Underground Tunnels.\>

✦ Follow the Troll King to the door of the mechanical room.

\<WATCH the Troll King open the door. You will need to know how to do it yourself.\>

\<See the false Troll King start the volcano. End chapter 4.\>

CHAPTER 5: VALANICE

\<See Valanice's silly trial cartoon. Get sentenced to horrible things unless you can put the moon back in the sky.\>

✦ Use Rosella's comb on the magic statuette in inventory.

\<See vision of Rosella in Ooga Booga.\>

\<Walk to the snake oil salesman's wagon.\>

✦ Click the magic statuette on the snake oil salesman to give it to him. Get the were-beast salve in return. Learn that you need animal hair to make it work.

\<Walk to the tree in the central plaza.\>

✦ Use the rubber chicken on the Y-shaped branch of the tree.

✦ Click the moon on the chicken attached to the branch to slingshot the moon.

<See the moon flung into the sky. >

<See archduke's congratulations cartoon.>

<Walk back to the woods. Walk to the edge of the were-woods.>

✦ Use the jackalope fur on the were-beast salve in inventory.

✦ Use the were-beast salve on Valanice.

<See Valanice turn into a jackalope cartoon. See Valanice running through the woods.>

<See swamp monster confront Valanice cartoon.>

<See Attis appear and save Valanice.>

<Make your way through the swamp to the gate of Ooga Booga.>

✦ Click on the gate of Ooga Booga land to go in.

<Walk to the deadfall. See the black cat. Learn that things are bad. Get suggestion to seek help from Etheria.>

<Walk to the burned-out mansion. See the barking dog.>

<Walk to the ghoul kids' treehouse.>

✦ Click on the elevator to go up to the treehouse.

✦ Click on the bone in the mummy's hand to take it.

✦ Click on the elevator to go back down from the treehouse.

<Walk back to the burned-out mansion.>

✦ Click the femur bone on the barking dog.

✦ Click on the dog to talk to him as often as you can.

\<Dog offers the Horseman's medal on his collar. Get medal.\>

\<Walk to the crypt where the Lady in Black is mourning.\>

✦ Use the medal on the Lady in Black. DO NOT just click on her.

\<See the Lady in Black clutch the medal to her heart and fly away.\>

\<Go east to the treehouse area. See ghoul kid tormenting the cat with firecrackers. He runs off and leaves a firecracker behind.\>

✦ Click on the firecracker to pick it up.

\<Walk back to the Horseman's crypt.\>

✦ Use the firecracker on the keyhole to jam it in.

\<Watch the door get blown open.\>

✦ Click on the door of the crypt to go in.

✦ Click on the sarcophagus to move the lid.

✦ Click on the open sarcophagus to take the skull.

\<Walk out of the crypt.\>

✦ Stand directly in the Horseman's path. As he charges toward you, use this skull on him.

\<See grateful Horseman cartoon. See reunion with his wife and dog. Get the use of the horse. Get the silver fife from the Horseman. See Valanice get on the horse, and the horse fly away.\>

\<Land in Etheria. See the horse leave.\>

\<Climb to the windy plateau on the mountain of winds.\>

✦ Click on the twisted tree to climb it.

✦ Click on ambrosia to take it.

✦ Click on the ground to climb back down.

<Walk to the dragonette meadow.>

✦ Use the ambrosia on the dragonettes to get one to come close.

<Listen carefully to the dragonette's song. See him eat the ambrosia.>

<Walk to the gazing ball in the garden.>

✦ Click on the strings to play the melody you just heard the dragonette singing.

✦ Click on the ball to enter and meet the Fates.

✦ Click on one of the Fates to talk to them. Learn that you must sleep to reach Mab and Dreamland.

<Walk to the Ooga Booga rainbow.>

✦ Click on the Ooga Booga rainbow to slide down.

<Walk to the Coroner's house.>

✦ Click on the Coroner's door to ask him about sleeping in his coffin. He says yes.

✦ Click on the coffin to lie down.

<See the Coroner pull the shroud over your face. See changing to Dreamland cartoon.>

<See journeying through dreamland cartoon.>

<See Mab frozen cartoon.>

<Wake up in the Coroner's house.>

<Exit the Coroner's house.>

✦ Use the fife on Valanice to call the horse.

<Ride the horse back to Etheria.>

\<Walk to the Three Fates' gazing ball.\>

✦ Play the melody on the harp.

✦ Click on the ball to enter.

✦ Click on one of the Fates to talk to them. Learn that Ceres is the only one who might know how to thaw Mab.

\<Walk to the woods rainbow.\>

✦ Click on the rainbow to slide down.

\<Walk to the cornucopia temple maiden.\>

✦ Click the ambrosia on the cornucopia.

\<Watch the cornucopia fill up.\>

✦ Click on the cornucopia to take a pomegranate.

\<Walk to the oak tree.\>

✦ Click the pomegranate on the oak tree.

\<See Ceres turn back into herself.\>

✦ Click on Ceres to talk to her. Learn that you need a crystal shaft filled with sunlight to thaw Mab. Learn that you can't travel to Dreamland carrying physical objects. She tells you to ask the Fates about it. Get hint about Malicia and crystals.

✦ Use the fife on Valanice to call the horse.

\<Ride back to Etheria.\>

✦ Click on the Ooga Booga rainbow to slide down.

\<Walk to the back of Malicia's house. Make sure the dog is not barking\>

✦ Click on the opening of the tunnel to crawl in.

<See cartoon of Valanice peeking up through the floorboards. Hear Malicia and the little dog coming in.>

✦ Click on the floorboards to duck back down.

<See Malicia getting ready for her big night. The little dog starts sniffing and digging at the knothole.>

✦ Use the ambrosia on the dog.

<See the dog chewing happily. Malicia picks him up and they leave.>

✦ Click on the knothole to push up the floorboards.

✦ Click on the room to come up out of the floor.

✦ Click on Malicia's lamp to take the crystal shaft.

✦ Click on the floorboards to exit Malicia's house.

✦ Use the fife on Valanice to call the horse.

<Ride to Etheria.>

<Walk to the Desert Rainbow.>

✦ Click on the rainbow to slide down.

<Walk to the stepped pyramid.>

<Enter the stepped pyramid.>

✦ Use the crystal shaft on the beam of light.

<See the crystal shaft fill up with sunlight.>

<Leave the temple.>

✦ Use the fife on Valanice to call the horse.

<Ride to Etheria.>

<Walk to the Three Fates' gazing ball.>

+ Click on the golden strings to play the key melody.

+ Click on the ball to enter.

+ Click on one of the Fates to talk to them. They tell you to seek the Dream Weaver. Get dream catcher.

<Walk to the Mountain of Winds.>

+ Climb the path to the Dream Weaver's cave.

<See the nightmare confront Valanice.>

+ Use the dream catcher on the nightmare.

+ Click on the Dream Weaver's cave to enter.

+ Click on the Dream Weaver to get his attention.

+ Click dream catcher on Dream Weaver to ask about getting to Dreamland. Find out that nightmares hate each other. Get tapestry of dreams.

+ Use tapestry of dreams on Valanice.

<See entering Dreamland cartoon. Get confronted by the Dreamland nightmare.>

+ Use the dream catcher on the Dreamland nightmare to release the Dream Weaver's nightmare.

+ Click on any exit arrow while the nightmares fight.

<Fall into the sea. See swimming cartoon.>

<Climb out onto the shore of Mab's Island.>

+ Click on doorway to enter Mab's temple.

+ Use crystal shaft with sunlight on Mab.

<See Mab thawing cartoon. Get magic bridle.>

ıb "zap" Valanice back to the waking land.>

<Walk to the Mountain of Winds.>

<Climb up to Sirocco's plateau.>

✦ Click on the wall, as far back from the edge as you can get.

✦ Click the bridle on Sirocco when he goes past.

<See riding Sirocco cartoon. Get attacked by Borasco. Fall to top of Mountain of Winds.>

<See Borasco and Gharbi cartoon. See Levanter cartoon.>

<See the winds go looking for Oberon and Titania. See time lapse. See Zephyr come back with Oberon and Titania.>

<See Oberon and Titania ride off. Valanice is stranded on the mountain. End of chapter 5.>

CHAPTER 6: ROSELLA

<See troll kings fighting cartoon.>

✦ Change the setting on the wand of transformation to "F" by clicking on the base of the handle in inventory close-up.

✦ Use the wand of transformation on the false Troll King. Look at them carefully. His eyes are green; the real Troll King's are purple.

<See the false Troll King turn into Edgar. Malicia comes bursting in, blasts the real Troll King, and blows Edgar away with a big wind. She zaps Rosella to a ledge inside the volcano.>

<See Rosella in the niche in the volcano cartoon. See Mab, Oberon, and Titania push the lava down.>

✦ Click the shovel on the wall behind Rosella to dig through.

<Walk to the mechanical room door.>

✦ Open the mechanical room side door by manipulating the face in the following order: left eye, right eye, nose.

<Go into the mechanical room.>

✦ IMPORTANT! Plug the Mysterious Device into its socket in the far left wall.

✦ Use the fragrant flower on the Troll King to awaken him.

<If you don't have the flower, go back out through the door. See the grating with the flower growing through.>

✦ Use the shovel on the stone in the wall to pry it loose.

✦ Click on the fallen stone to stand on it.

<See Rosella take the flower.>

<Hurry back to the mechanical room.>

✦ Open the mechanical room door.

✦ Click the flower on the Troll King to awaken him.

<See the Troll King get up and shut off the volcano.>

<See Valanice, Edgar, and Mathilda burst in. Happy Reunion cartoon.>

<See Malicia show up. She and Edgar have a magical duel, and Edgar is killed.>

✦ Click on the Mysterious Device on the wall to unplug it.

✦ Use the device on Malicia to turn her into a baby.

✦ Use the black cat's extra life on Edgar to resurrect him.

<See ending cartoon. Game over, man, game over!>

Backstories and Legends

EDGAR AND LOLOTTE

Edgar was born the son of Oberon and Titania, King and Queen of the Faeries. When he was just a baby, an evil faerie named Lolotte was cast from Etheria for treachery and wicked deeds. She was so furious that she concocted a scheme to steal the baby prince from his home. Once she had him, she changed his appearance and called him her own. Oberon and Titania searched the world for their baby, but finally they had to give up and turn their attentions back to their kingdom. They thought their only son was dead.

THE FALL OF MALICIA (HOW COUNT TSEPISH LOST HIS HEAD)

Many years back, Malicia, who is the sister of Titania, hatched a terrible plot to overthrow Etheria. With a band of fanatical followers, she tried to seize power from Oberon and Titania in a vicious attack on the castle. Oberon and Titania fought valiantly, and all of the guardians of Faerieland rose to defend them. All of the rebels were slain or cast from Etheria except for Malicia, who fought like a demon and would not give up. She was dealt a terrible blow by Count Tsepish of Ooga Booga land. His true strike allowed Oberon and Titania to defeat Malicia, but before they could subdue her,

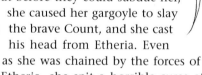

she caused her gargoyle to slay the brave Count, and she cast his head from Etheria. Even as she was chained by the forces of Etheria, she spit a horrible curse after the Count. He rose to haunt Ooga Booga as the Headless Horseman, his bride Elspeth died of a broken heart, and his faithful hound stayed with his mansion even as it was burned to the ground by the Boogeyman, who had collaborated with Malicia all along. The three ghosts were forever cursed to occupy the same land, but to be cruelly kept apart for all eternity.

EDGAR AND MALICIA

After Edgar was changed back into his normal body by Genesta at the end of *King's Quest IV*, word quickly spread that there was a strange and noble young faerie of great power living alone on the shores of Tamir. Oberon and Titania dared not hope that it was their son, but they went to meet the young man for themselves. They were overjoyed to discover that it was their long lost boy after all. They brought him back to Etheria amid great celebration and ceremony. They had a glittering party for him that very evening. What Oberon and Titania didn't know was that Malicia, who had been stripped of her powers and cast from Etheria many years before, had built her power back up to a terrifying level. She kidnapped Edgar from the gardens of Etheria in the middle of the celebration, changing his form to look like the Troll King, whom she had just imprisoned in Ooga Booga land. Her evil scheme not only gained her an impostor Troll King to act as her puppet, but effectively got rid of Oberon and Titania as well. She left false clues and rumors that led them to think their son had been kidnapped by an evil wind. They set out to search for him immediately, and Malicia was free to enact her terrible plot.

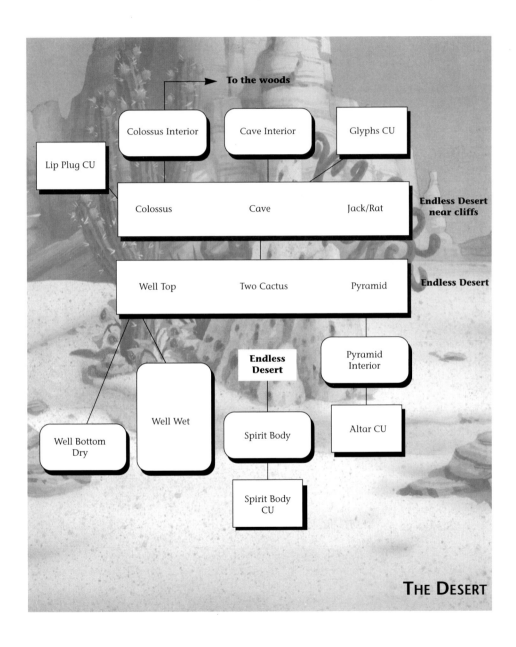

To the woods

Colossus Interior   Cave Interior   Glyphs CU

Lip Plug CU

Colossus   Cave   Jack/Rat   **Endless Desert near cliffs**

Well Top   Two Cactus   Pyramid   **Endless Desert**

Endless Desert   Pyramid Interior

Well Wet

Well Bottom Dry   Spirit Body   Altar CU

Spirit Body CU

THE DESERT

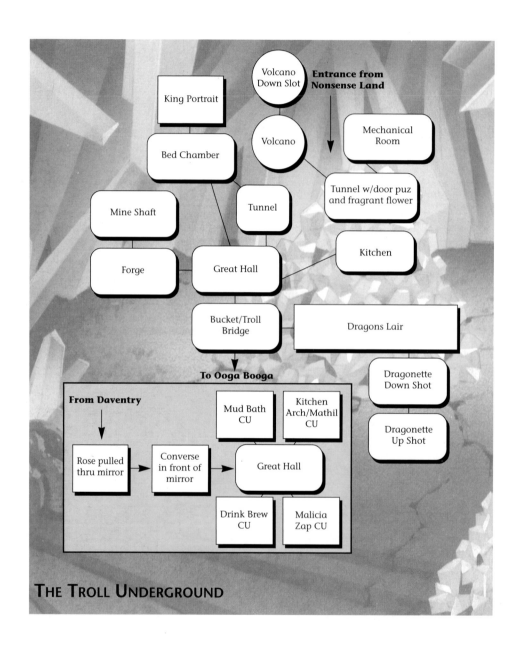

THE TROLL UNDERGROUND

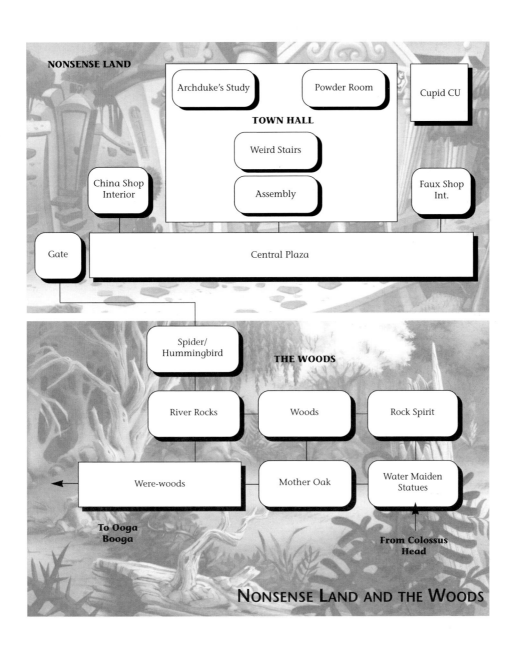

NONSENSE LAND

Archduke's Study

Powder Room

Cupid CU

TOWN HALL

Weird Stairs

China Shop Interior

Assembly

Faux Shop Int.

Gate

Central Plaza

Spider/ Hummingbird

THE WOODS

River Rocks

Woods

Rock Spirit

Were-woods

Mother Oak

Water Maiden Statues

To Ooga Booga

From Colossus Head

NONSENSE LAND AND THE WOODS

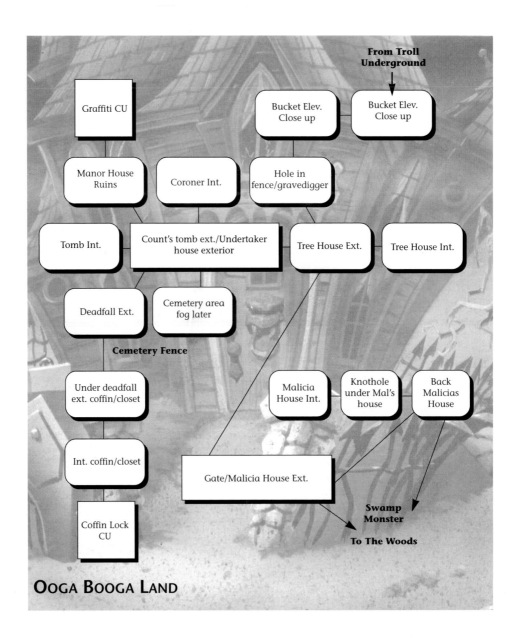

From Troll Underground

Graffiti CU

Bucket Elev. Close up

Bucket Elev. Close up

Manor House Ruins

Coroner Int.

Hole in fence/gravedigger

Tomb Int.

Count's tomb ext./Undertaker house exterior

Tree House Ext.

Tree House Int.

Deadfall Ext.

Cemetery area fog later

Cemetery Fence

Under deadfall ext. coffin/closet

Malicia House Int.

Knothole under Mal's house

Back Malicias House

Int. coffin/closet

Gate/Malicia House Ext.

Swamp Monster

Coffin Lock CU

To The Woods

OOGA BOOGA LAND

Gazing Ball

Flying to top of Mountain of Winds

Top, Mountain of Winds

Garden under floating castle

Dream weavers cave ext.

Int. Dream weavers cave

Rainbows/Entrance to Etheria

Meadow

Base of Mountain of Winds

Desert • Ooga Boogo • Woods • Falderal

Monster Chase

Dream Sea

Mab Island ext.

Mab Temple Int.

Mab on Ice CU

ETHERIA

Credits

DESIGNED BY
Lorelei Shannon
Roberta Williams

WRITTEN BY
Lorelei Shannon

DIRECTORS
Andy Hoyos
Lorelei Shannon
Roberta Williams

PRODUCER
Mark Seibert

ART DIRECTOR
Andy Hoyos

DIRECTOR OF ANIMATION
Marc Hudgins

LEAD PROGRAMMERS
Oliver Brelsford
Henry Yu

MUSICIANS
Neal Grandstaff
Dan Kehler
Mark Seibert
Jay Usher

VOICE DIRECTOR
Lorelei Shannon

QUALITY ASSURANCE LEAD
Dan Woolard

IN-HOUSE ANIMATION - CHAPTER 6
Steven Gregory
Sherry Wheeler
Jason Zayas

IN-HOUSE COMPUTER INK & PAINT
Darvin Atkeson
Maria Fruehe
Desi Hartman
Karin Nestor
Frankie Powell
Donovan Skirvin
Donald Waller
Phy Williams
Chris Willis
Deanna Yhalkee

BACKGROUND LAYOUT
Darlou Gams
Terry Robinson

BACKGROUND ILLUSTRATION
Dennis Durrell
Darrin Fuller
Darlou Gams
Terry Robinson

BACKGROUND STYLING
Dennis Durrell

BACKGROUND COLOR KEYS
Darlou Gams
Terry Robinson

CHARACTER DESIGNS
Marc Hudgins

SUMMER INTERNS
Nicole Berg
Steven Gregory
Karena Kliefoth
Neil Krivoski
Tracy Wagner

3D INVENTORY OBJECTS
Jon Bock
Rich Powell
Donald Waller

SGI ANIMATION & EFFECTS
Kim White

PROGRAMMERS
Dave Artis
Vana Baker
Arijit De
Tom DeSalvo
Carlos Escobar
Robert Lindsley
Michael Litton
Randy McNeill
Sean Mooney
Doug Oldfield
Kevin Ray
Jerry Shaw
Henry Yu

SYSTEM PROGRAMMERS
Ed Critchlow
Day Foy

J. Mark Hood
Ken Koch
Terry McHenry
Larry Scott
Chris Smith
Greg Tomko-Pavia

ADDITIONAL QA
Robin Bradley
Mike Brosius
Joe Carper
Judy Crites
Jon Meek
Leonard Salas

CONFIGURATION GROUP
Roger Clendenning
Dave Clingman
John Cunney
Bill Davis, Jr.
Lynne Dayton
Ken Eaton
Mike Jones
Mike Pickhinke
John Ratcliffe
Sharon Simmons
John Trauger
Doug Wheeler

**MUSIC FOR MOVIE
SEQUENCES SCORED BY**
Mark Seibert
Jay Usher

**OPENING SONG
"A LAND BEYOND DREAMS"**
Written by: Jay Usher
Lyric by: Lorelei Shannon
Sung by: Debbie Seibert

SOUND EFFECTS AND AUDIO WORK
Neal Grandstaff
Kelli Spurgeon
Rick Spurgeon
Jay Usher

VOICE CASTING AND DIRECTION
Lorelei Shannon

VOICE AUDITIONS
Taylor Korobow
Casting Works

Fantasy Studios
Studio Engineer
Eric Tompson

DREAMS SOFTWARE OPERATOR
Dan Kehler

ANIMATION HOUSES

Animation Magic Inc.
Chapter 1 and Global Animation
Animation
Kostya Biryukov, Anton Chizhov,
Tanya Demidova, Ksana Giotova,
Katya Gorelova, Katya Kruglova,
Ilya Maximov, Marina Mikheeva,
Sasha Naoumova, Andrey Pugachev,
Oksana Romanova, Lena Rumyantseva,
Lena Savik, Katya Vassilyeva,
Alice Vizirova, Natasha Yakovleva,
Masha Yakushina, Ira Zheleznova
Digital Ink & Paint
Marina Aksenova, Oksana Bilan,
Tanya Fedotova, Denis Goroshkov,
Kristina Kim, Alexey Konkin,
Vera Korolova, Tanya Krasavina,
Alina Kudryashova, Sasha Myala,
Sasha Sakov, Olga Sumenko,
Tanya Tavrueva, Ira Yershova
Technical Assistants
Denis Ivanov, Tanya Smirnova,
Tanya Shalygina, Tom Faiano
Background Paintings
Volodya Karnaoukhov,
Nadya Obedkova, Kostya Kossarev,
Ira Shostik
Production Management
Boris Bigouleav, Lena Beloborodova,
Dale DeSharone, Sasha Makarov,
Lyuba Nedeorezova, Igor Razboff,
Alesy Yeseyev

LA West Film Production
Chapter 4 and 6
Director of Animation
Ivan Tomicic
Animators
Stjepan Bartolic, Zvonimir Cuk,
Darko Krec, Neven Petricic,
Esad Ribic, Goran Sudzuka
Inbetweening & Cleaning
Marina Hruskar, Damir Jurisic,
Maja Surjak, Vlasta Zubcevic

Animation Checking
Esad Ribic
Scanning
Nenad Baljak, Rikard Blazicko,
Bojan Hrabar, Jadran Zdunic
Digital Ink & Paint
Jadranka Brecak, Andreas Cogelja,
Sandra Grgec, Marija Ivsic,
Denis Lepur, Sinisa Matijasic,
Lovorka Ostovic, Robert Seruga,
Suncica Spriovan, Tatjana Trgovec,
Timomir Vlajic, Zelko Vlajic

Dungeon Ink & Paint
Chapter 2, 3 and 5
Animators
Frank Barnhill, John Beam,
Kellie Dover, Chad Frye,
Preston Jones, Mike Knobl,
Bill Morris, David E. Rogers,
Stan White
Inbetweeners/Cleanup Artists
Tracy J. Blackwell, Kevin E. Davis,
Jason Gammon, Jeffrey D. Hayes,
Dungeon Ink & Paint
David Ellis, Lisa Ellis, Mary Fulton,
Tony Lavender, Lori Pinera,
Angelique Ruff, Traci Scruggs,
Paula Stacy
Production Assistants
Beth A. Hopping,
Michael L. Honeycutt Jr.,
Shane White, Kristi Wood
Thanks
Beth Hopping

Animotion
Chapter 5 -
Opening & Closing Movies
Director of Animation
David Hicock
Production Supervisor
Larry Royer
Creative Supervision
David Hicock, Larry Royer,
Bob Switalski
Key Animation
David Gilbert, David Hicock,
Larry Royer, Apryl Knobbe Young,
Assistant Animation
David Bleich, Jim Burns,
Donna Campbell, Mike Carter,
Aaron McDowell, Mike Feather,
Marcus Gregory, Leslie Jaye,

John Larkin, Joseph Larkin,
Alan Nash, Jennifer Robin,
Johnny Robinson
Additional Animation
Dennis Kennedy
Technical Consultants
Steve Bogdonovich, Dick Moody
Digital Ink and Paint
Steve Bogdonovich, Ron Cleveland,
Chip G. Hartford, Robert Leonard,
Aaron Moody, Dick Moody,
Michele Moody, Jonathan C. Parker
Paint Coordinator
Dick Moody

Voice Talent -
Our Heroines, Heroes and Villains
Rosella: Maureen McVerry
Valanice: Carol Bach y Rita
Malicia: Ruth Kobart
Edgar/False Troll King: Jesse Moises
King Otar Fenris III,
Lord of the Trolls: Denny Delk
Cuddles: Roger Jackson
In the Desert
The Kangaroo Rat: Roger Jackson
The Desert Spirit: Fred Barson
The Jackalope: Jeffry O'Brien
In the Vulcanix Underground
Mathilde: Esther Hirsch
The Rude Forging Troll: Jeffry O'Brien
The Jeweler Troll: Joe Paulino
The Troll Cook: Jim Cranna
Brutus the Bridge Troll: Don Robins
The Crystal Dragon: Ruth Kobart
Male Mud Bath Troll 1: Greg Walsh
Male Mud Bath Troll 2: Marcus Lewis
Female Mud Bath Troll 1:
Maureen McVerry
Female Mud Bath Troll 2: Esther Hirsch
The Dragon Toad: Greg Walsh
Spike: Carol Bach y Rita
Spike's Mother: Jeffry O'Brien
In the Woods
Attis/Attis the Stag: Toby Gleason
Ceres: Carol Bach y Rita
The Hummingbird: Maureen McVerry
The Spider: Joe Paulino
The Rock Spirit: Tim White

In the Swamp
  The Three-Headed Carnivorous Plant:
  Roger Jackson, Roger Jackson and
  Roger Jackson Wow!
In the Falderal
  The Obnoxious Gate Guard: Doug Boyd
  archduke Fifi le YipYap: Jim Cranna
  Chicken Petite: Esther Hirsch
  The Mockingbird: Jim Cranna
  The Bull in the China Shop: Jarion Monroe
  The Snake Oil Salesman: Roger Jackson
  Treasure the China Bird: Maureen McVerry
  Ersatz the Faux Shop Owner: Toby Gleason
  Town Hall Door Guard: Simon Vance
  Arresting Badger Guard: Simon Vance
  Badgers of the Jury: Fred Barson, Doug Boyd,
    Jim Cranna,Denny Delk
  The Magic Statuette: Ruth Kobart
In OogaBooga Land
  The Coroner: Marcus Lewis
  Ghoul Kid 1: Roger Jackson
  Ghoul Kid 2: Yukiko Yamaguchi
  The Gravedigger: Marcus Lewis
  The Black Cat: Yukiko Yamaguchi
  The Black Dog: Jesse Moises
  Count Tsepish (The Headless Horseman):
    Joe Paulino
  Lady Tsepish (The Woman in Black):
    Willow Wray
  The Boogeyman: Don Robins
  The Shrunken Heads: Doug Boyd,
    Jim Cranna, Denny Delk,
  The Mummy: Fred Barson
  Mr. Nibbler the Psycho Mouse:
    Joe Paulino
  Mr. Bugbear (Dr. Cadaver's Patient):
    Jeffry O'Brien
In Etheria
  Lachesis: Willow Wray
  Clotho: Carol Bach y Rita
  Atropos: Yukiko Yamaguchi
  Borasco: Don Robins
  Gharbi: Willow Wray
  Levanter: Toby Gleason
  Oberon: Timothy White
  Titania: Carol Bach y Rita

Paymaster
Talent Fund

Special Thanks To
Tammy Dargan, Casey Jones,
Robin Kleeman, Al Lowe, Mom,
Marie Salerno, Joni Williamson

Hintbook Design
Lori Lucia

Notes